THE
MONTHLY
GIVING
Mastermind

THE
MONTHLY
GIVING
Mastermind

A FRAMEWORK TO
BUILD, GROW, & SUSTAIN
SUBSCRIPTIONS FOR GOOD

Dana Snyder

To my rae of sunshine, Kennedy:

You are my greatest gift. You inspire me every day with your boundless curiosity and joy.

To Daniel:

Your unwavering encouragement and love have been my rock.

To my parents:

Your belief in my dreams and constant support have been the foundation of my journey.

To you, the reader—your dedication, passion, and relentless drive make a difference every single day.

Keep shining your light.

FOREWORD

by Gloria Umanah,
Founder & CEO of the Hope Booth

IF YOU FIND what you love AND what you're good at, you've found **your passion**.

If you find what you're good at AND what you can be paid for, you've found **your profession**.

If you can find what you can be paid for AND what the world needs, you've found **your vocation**.

If you can find what the world needs AND what you love, you've found **your mission**.

But there's one more category: a Japanese concept called Ikigai.

It is the intersectionality of the work you long to do and the work the world needs you to do. Most people spend their entire lives searching for their Ikigai because at the core, we all desire to discover our reason, our because, and our purpose for being alive.

If you're reading this right now, you've more than likely discovered your Ikigai; the burning passion and conviction that sets your heart on fire with no permission or precaution.

It was in the Summer of 2020 during the global pandemic when I read one statistic that would forever change my life.

"The average person living on the streets goes 3-6 months without being looked in the eye."

It was almost as if the words seared themselves onto my heart in an instant. They were forever stuck with me no matter how hard I tried to dismiss them. My devotion had no plan of deviation, until the moment I read those words and a sudden burden of responsibility followed.

I wondered for quite some time why there was such a great weight on my shoulders after reading that statistic and a year later it clicked; it was because I too was awfully familiar with the feeling of invisibility.

On October 29, 2011 I almost lost my life to suicide because I was acquainted with the weight of feeling unseen, but I'm here today because of the power of one four lettered word, hope. It dawned on me at that moment, that regardless if you're living on the streets or if you're the CFO of a Fortune 500, mental health doesn't discriminate. It's no respecter of persons, place, position, or power. Everyone deserves to be seen, and perhaps that truth accompanied by hope would save the 900,000,000 lives affected by mental health struggles around the globe.

This is what led to the creation of The Hope Booth; an evidence based interactive immersive experience designed to spread hope and connect people to local help and support in the form of reimagined telephone booths installed around the globe, offering hope and help 24/7 free of charge. The Hope Booth is pioneering a new way forward to combat the mental health crisis and I believe in my lifetime we will see a global movement where no one goes unseen, and I have committed my life to being a part of that story, alongside our ever-growing global monthly donor community, The Movement.

Without the continuous support of The Movement, we would not have the opportunity to make our mission a reality and see lives forever transformed at a sustainable rate. Truth be told, establishing The Movement was the most monumental decision our organization could have made and my only regret is that we didn't begin sooner. Because one way or another, we've all had or will have the daunting realization that the story we have committed our lives to is bigger than us as individuals. If there's anything I know to be true, it's that movements require invitations.

But let me warn you; if we aren't careful, the concept of building a movement can plague us with intimidation if we don't recognize the power of an invitation.

This work can't be done alone.

Find the people whose hearts beat for your cause and encourage them to run on mission with you; perhaps your invitation into the meaningful and life changing work you're committed to is the doorway to someone else's Ikigai discovery, to be a part of change in this world.

Together, we not only *can* go further, but we *will* go further and faster, for the sake of others. It's guaranteed.

So if there's anything you hear from me; begin today and if you've already begun, please don't give up. There are lives dependent on your commitment to the good, hard, worthy cause you are fighting for.

CONTENTS

INTRODUCTION

DO YOU EVER FEEL the relentless grind to find new supporters, anxiously holding your breath as you await responses to grant submissions, grappling with the intense pressure of organizing major events, and praying that your top donors will come through? It can be a lot to handle, and sometimes it feels like no matter how hard you work, it's never *quite enough* to meet your organization's never-ending goals.

You got into nonprofit work because you wanted to make a difference. You saw a need in the world and felt compelled to address it, to bring about positive change. Whether it's helping those in need, advocating for a cause you're passionate about, or working towards a better future, your heart led you to this path. Your role directly impacts lives and contributes to a greater good, but the reality of the day-to-day can sometimes feel overwhelming.

If this feels familiar to you, know that you're not alone.

Nonprofits are not only the heartbeat of our communities but also a major economic force, employing over twelve million people and spending nearly $2 trillion annually. According to the 2024 Giving USA Report, nonprofits generated an impressive $557.16 billion in support in 2023, with individual donors contributing a significant 67% of that total. This underscores the crucial role that individual giving plays not only in advancing nonprofit missions but also in bolstering the economy in numerous ways.

However, if you're in the nonprofit world, you know it's not easy.

With tight budgets, rising costs, and the ever-present issue of staff burnout, it feels like the challenges keep piling up. It's a tough environment, and it's getting harder to keep up with the increasing demands and often limited resources.

What if there was a way to ease that burden and the feeling of burnout to create a reliable stream of income that you could count on month after month?

What if you could shift your focus from constantly searching for new donors to building deeper relationships with the ones you already have?

That's where recurring giving comes in.

A steady, predictable stream of income helps you manage cash flow and plan long-term projects more effectively. Monthly giving programs do just that. They not only provide financial stability for operations but also help build stronger connections with your donors. So, instead of constantly scrambling for funds, you can focus on what really matters: making a lasting impact with the supporters who believe in your mission. It's a game changer for any nonprofit looking to sustain and grow its efforts without burning out.

Sounds like a dream, right?!

But it doesn't have to be just a dream. It's the reality for many organizations that have prioritized monthly giving as a necessary part of their fundraising efforts. Recurring donations can make a significant change in how you manage your resources, plan your programs, and ultimately, achieve your mission.

Over the past five years, foundations have contributed $493 billion, while individuals have collectively donated an astounding $1.9 trillion. This striking difference highlights the unparalleled impact of individual donors in modern philanthropy. Loyal, ongoing supporters are the true drivers of nonprofit success, underscoring the importance of cultivating and maintaining these vital relationships.

With that said, this book isn't just about sharing a framework to grow your monthly donors; **it's about transforming YOUR work.** To start your day without feeling ten steps behind before you take your first sip of coffee. To shift from a reactive, stress-filled approach to a proactive, positive, and strategic mindset.

If you're feeling the weight of burnout, **this book is your guide to reclaiming your passion and purpose.** It's designed to help you build a sustainable, reliable revenue stream that eases the constant pressure of fundraising. You'll learn practical strategies and actionable steps to cultivate a loyal base of monthly donors, enabling you to plan ahead with confidence and peace of mind.

Imagine having the freedom to focus on what truly matters—your mission and the impact you want to make. No more endless cycles of chasing new donors or worrying about meeting financial goals. Instead, you'll have the tools and knowledge to create a thriving monthly giving program that supports your organization's growth and stability.

This transformation starts here, with this book.

For me, my transformation and fascination for monthly giving all started by being a donor.

When I moved to Los Angeles in 2017, I was introduced to the incredible mission of Dressember.[1] I was struck by the powerful message behind their mission, which combined fashion and creativity with advocacy to combat human trafficking. After watching the founder's TED Talk, "How A Dress Can Change The World" by Blythe Hill on YouTube, I started following their work on Instagram.

As I delved deeper into my research, I learned about the staggering revenue generated by this heinous crime. I discovered that two-thirds of the $150 billion generated by human trafficking annually comes from commercial sexual exploitation. This shocking statistic only reinforced my belief that constant support was necessary to make a significant impact.

---

1   Dressember is now an official program under the International Justice Mission, and I'm thrilled for this partnership to combine resources and make a significant impact together! As of April 1, 2024, all contributions to Dressember will directly support the work of IJM and its partner organizations around the globe.

Let's turn that dream into your *everyday reality.*

A one-time donation or participating in a single fundraising event wouldn't be enough. Have you ever felt this way about an organization you support?

After following their work for a couple of years, I wanted to become a consistent and dedicated supporter of Dressember's mission. From their emails and social posts, I learned the organization had launched a monthly giving program called The Collective—*you'll hear about this later in the book*—and I wanted to play a long-term part in their efforts.

I've been part of The Collective since 2021. For me, it wasn't just about making a monthly donation; it was about being part of a bigger community of advocates. I knew my recurring gift of $25 would mean so much more compounded by the efforts of a larger group.

The community includes people from all walks of life, united by the belief that every individual has the power to make a positive impact in the world. As I learned more about Dressember's work through The Collective, I was able to see firsthand the impact that consistent support could make in creating a better world for all. It not only allowed me to support Dressember's mission, but it also gave me a sense of purpose and belonging.

It's through The Collective that I've seen the extreme benefit monthly giving provides nonprofits. Anytime I look to give, I always search for the opportunity to contribute to their monthly giving program as a recurring-first donor.

In parallel, working as a digital marketing consultant for nonprofits, my interest in monthly giving only grew stronger, and I was filled with questions:

➜ Why don't all organizations have monthly giving programs?
➜ Who is doing it successfully?
➜ What technology platforms are available to help scale and grow recurring gifts?
➜ And what kind of team is needed to run a successful program?

These questions consumed me.

I wanted to know what made certain programs thrive, so I became a "secret shopper" of monthly giving programs by studying their website, making a small, monthly gift, and taking note of the communications I received following the initial gift and every month after. This allowed me to gain a deeper understanding of the key elements that contribute to a successful program, where I felt seen as a donor, and where there were gaps.

I realized when there were gaps it was mostly due to the bandwidth and resource limitations. I get it—finding the time to build a program, optimizing the donation experience for recurring giving, going through the process of researching outside help for website design, copywriting, and graphic design sounds daunting before you even begin, let alone finding the time to make it happen! That's why creating a monthly giving program ends up staying on so many to-do lists for years and years.

Something needed to change to make this easier. To find a way to make creating a successful monthly giving program more accessible to organizations of all sizes to bring in more sustainable funds and a diverse donor base for the health of the sector.

It was also around this time that I wrapped up participating in an incredible business mastermind experience for myself (*more to come on this!*), and throughout that program, I would receive my monthly email from The Collective with Dressember's program updates.

A big idea began to emerge. **What if there was a mastermind program for nonprofits?**

A small group container where they could learn how to build successful monthly giving programs with their peers? I couldn't shake this idea, and slowly, it started to take shape.

As I continued digital marketing work with my clients and led countless webinars, I couldn't help but feel the urge to introduce organizations to one another. I found myself saying, "You need to meet x," and "I wish you could see what x is doing!" It made me wonder, what if organizations weren't working alone but learning and growing together just like I had in my mastermind?

So with an idea of a monthly giving framework in mind, I assembled a team of experts I trusted—a website designer, copywriter, graphic designer, and video editor—and launched the Monthly Giving Mastermind. The first group consisted of six nonprofits from across the US ready to create or improve their recurring giving programs.

Over four months together, not only did these programs come to life, but the community and conversations within the group were invaluable for everyone involved. Nearly every testimonial included appreciation and support of going through the process together. That was the beautiful part of the mastermind experience. Every hurdle, frustration, celebration, and AHA moment was able to be shared with each other.

It was a truly magical experience!

During this time, I also launched my podcast, *Missions to Movements*, and continued to hear story after story of how recurring giving completely shifted the energy and progress of organizations.

Fast forward to present day, through hundreds of interviews, many conferences, and creating over a dozen monthly giving programs, I developed a 5-Step Framework to build, grow, and sustain a thriving recurring giving program. These steps or essential elements are not simply theories but rather tried-and-true methods that have been proven to work.

Through this book, YOU are invited to be part of the Monthly Giving Mastermind.

While a solid 5-Step Framework is essential, it's the real-life stories that truly bring each step to life.

A mastermind is so powerful because the people in the group are willing to be open, transparent, and vulnerable to share their challenges and solutions with the fellow participants.

I was part of a mastermind experience in 2021 that changed everything for me. The concept involves bringing together a group of like-minded individuals who are committed to helping each other achieve their goals. The idea is to create a collaborative and supportive environment where members can share their knowledge, experiences, and resources. This collective wisdom and support can accelerate personal and professional growth, providing participants with insights and perspectives they might not gain on their own.

Throughout this book, **you are invited** to become part of the mastermind composed of fifteen organizations of all sizes. These organizations have generously shared behind-the-scenes insights into how their recurring giving programs operate to illustrate how each step looks in practice, aiming to uplift the entire sector.

Whether you're just starting out or have twenty-five years of experience, run a small one-person shop or have a team of 250, focus on hyper-local support or global efforts, you'll find valuable insights throughout these pages. The organizations I'm about to introduce are filled with gems that will inspire and guide you on your journey.

Here's a sneak peek into the stories, learnings, and insights you're about to hear...

1. **charity: water** has one of the most renowned monthly giving programs praised and idolized by many, but how did one video catapult giving, and what's driven continuous success?

2. **Dressember** operated as a seasonal peer-to-peer fundraising campaign for years. How did they merge the gap and introduce a swell of monthly giving support?

3. **Because International's** rebranding efforts led to a jump in regular givers. We'll discuss this campaign and the future of where they want to go.

4. **Feeding Westchester** generated support from leadership and took a chance on face-to-face fundraising efforts that paid off!

5. **Miry's List** is a prime example of an organization that understood the need for recurring giving based on the needs of their supporters.

6. **The Adventure Project's** initial monthly giving campaign launch brought in one hundred donors! We'll review how and what the program looks like today.

7. **Brown Bagging for Calgary's Kids** has built a beautiful twelve-month-and-beyond retention strategy. We'll explore each month and the special moments created with supporters.

8. **The Water Project** has created a strong regular donor community that participates in annual upsell campaigns each year. What's the secret to their success?

9. **Daily Giving** leads with a profound recurring-first approach. Does it work, and how do they deal with donor churn?

10. **The Tim Tebow Foundation** was feeling stagnant in the growth of their regular giving and explored a new marketing strategy that grew their recurring donors from 6,500 to 20,000+ in a year! How!?

11. **IJM UK** dialed into marketing efforts to find passionate believers in their mission and activated a brand new approach to communications. Did it work?

12. **Queer Women of Color Media Arts Project** shares how your existing superfans can take the reins to grow your monthly supporters for you.

13. **The Hope Booth** realized a massive missed opportunity by not starting with a recurring-first focus when they first launched their organization. How have they turned the corner?

14. **Chamber of Mothers** is proof of the importance of giving your program a name to call in the believers and retract the doubters.

15. **Roots Ethiopia** had a monthly giving program that sat idle for years until they went through a major transformation that put recurring on the map and became a crucial part of their fundraising efforts.

This book highlights their achievements, the missions, and the people that make it all possible because if we're going to solve some of the biggest problems of our time, it's going to happen by coming together!

THROUGH THIS MASTERMIND, YOU'LL LEARN HOW TO:

1. Create a product that resonates with donors
2. Make the giving process easy
3. Call upon supporters to spread the word

4. Make the ask in creative ways

5. Express gratitude and joy to supporters

Each of these steps is crucial in building a successful program, and the information shared in this book is a tool for anyone looking to make a difference in their organization through monthly giving.

Let this book be a starting point to sharing our findings with one another so together we can all achieve more impact.

Ready to get started? Let's set the stage...

PART ONE

CHAPTER 1

Setting the Stage: Foundations of Monthly Giving

WELCOME TO YOUR new job as Chief Evangelist of Regular Giving.

OK, definitely just made that up and it doesn't mean you have a whole new job description, but to have a recurring program succeed, you have to be unapologetically ALL IN.

And not just you...

Before the fun begins, it's important to understand two foundational elements of building a successful recurring giving program:

1. Convincing leadership
2. Having an accountability partner or community for support

One of the biggest hurdles I see with making monthly giving a priority is buy-in from leadership. It's a *whole lot more fun* to build a monthly giving program with the support of your leadership team. Getting leadership buy-in should be a top priority. When leaders are on board, they feel a sense of ownership and accountability for the program's success. They can provide valuable insights and guidance to shape the program, ensuring it aligns with the organization's overall mission and values.

If this is you, nodding your head, I've been in those meetings too. Those meetings where it feels like no matter what you say, there's a brick wall up to any new ideas. I felt this mini chapter was necessary to help get over that hurdle. If you need help convincing leadership that having a monthly giving program is not just a nice-to-have but necessary to diversify your revenue stream with a sustainable giving model... I have some ideas!

What if your leadership (*or you*) is already bought in? Great! Skip down to the second essential building block.

FOUNDATIONAL ELEMENT #1: CONVINCING LEADERSHIP

Here's three strategies for you.

Imagine you are a nonprofit professional named Sam. Sam works tirelessly at their organization, Hope for All, which provides critical resources to underserved communities. Despite the organization's impactful work, Sam often feels the financial strain during off-peak fundraising periods. They know there's a better way to sustain their mission and decide to propose a monthly giving program to the leadership team. Here's how they craft their narrative.

Scene 1: The Predictable Revenue Stream

Sam sits down with the leadership team, a group of dedicated yet cautious individuals, and starts by painting a picture of the current financial landscape.

"Every year, we face a roller coaster of income," Sam begins. "Our annual campaigns bring in a significant surge of funds, but once the excitement fades, we're left navigating the calm, uncertain waters until the next big fundraiser."

They lean forward, eyes bright with excitement. "But what if I told you there's a way to ensure we have a steady stream of income all year round? A way that allows us to plan and budget more effectively?"

Sam explains how a monthly giving program can smooth out these financial peaks and valleys, providing consistent revenue that makes budgeting and resource allocation much easier. "Imagine knowing that every month, we have a reliable amount of money coming in. We could tackle long-term projects with confidence, knowing we have the funds to see them through."

Sam cites the 2024 Neon One Recurring Giving Report: Data-Backed Insights for Sustainable Generosity, noting that the retention rate for monthly donors is around 78%, compared to just 38% for one-time donors. "This isn't just about money," they emphasize. "It's about stability and planning for the future with certainty."

Scene 2: Increased Donor Lifetime Value

Next, Sam shifts the focus to the donors themselves. "Now, let's talk about our supporters," they say, pulling up a slide showing a graph of donor contributions.

"Did you know that monthly donors tend to give more over time than one-time donors?" they ask. "A $20 monthly donation might seem small, but it adds up to $240 a year – much more than our average one-time gift."

Sam shares data from Classy.org, which indicates that recurring donors give 42% more annually than one-time donors. "This means our donors are not only more loyal, but they also contribute more over their lifetime."

Sam tells the story of a donor named Emily who started giving $10 a month a year ago. "Emily feels a deeper connection to our cause because she's contributing regularly. She's more engaged, attends our events, and even brought her friends to volunteer with us."

Scene 3: Enhanced Donor Retention and Relationship Building

Finally, Sam brings it all home by talking about relationships. "One of the most powerful aspects of a monthly giving program is the relationships we build with our donors."

Sam describes how regular communication with monthly donors fosters a stronger emotional bond. "When we update our donors monthly, they feel more involved and appreciated. This continuous interaction builds trust and loyalty."

Sam highlights that organizations with strong monthly giving programs report higher donor satisfaction and loyalty. "Imagine sending personalized messages, celebrating anniversaries, and sharing exclusive updates with our most committed supporters. This isn't just fundraising; it's building a community."

The Wrap Up: A Vision for the Future

Sam wraps up the presentation, looks around the room at the thoughtful faces of colleagues, and says, "Implementing a monthly giving program isn't just a nice-to-have. It's essential for diversifying our revenue stream, increasing donor lifetime value, and fostering deeper relationships with our supporters."

Sam smiles, feeling hopeful. "Let's build a future where we're not just surviving between campaigns but thriving with the ongoing support of a community that believes in our mission as much as we do."

With these compelling stories and evidence-backed arguments, Sam successfully convinces the leadership team to embrace the idea of a monthly giving program, setting Hope for All on a path to greater stability and impact.

Go Sam!

If you need extra ideas for the conversation, let this book be your resource to pull stats and examples from. By the end of your conversation, I hope this makes it a no-brainer!

Now, if you're the leader (*you got this!*), surround yourself with people that are just a step ahead of you to learn and get support from. This was the power of the mastermind I was in.

I was SO excited to be around other people who were dealing with the same challenges I was. But the mastermind only lasted for a year, and I didn't want to feel alone again.

FOUNDATIONAL ELEMENT #2: FIND ACCOUNTABILITY PARTNERS OR A COMMUNITY OF PEERS

Whether it's through a community I've created or friends in the industry, being part of a group that has supported and challenged me along this wild journey of being an entrepreneur has been invaluable.

One example of this in action is a Slack channel that exists for nonprofit consultants. As a solopreneur, I eagerly joined this community of peers. Sometimes you just want feedback on an email you've drafted or to get eyes on a new website you're working on. In our Slack group, there's even a #publishing channel where I shared ideas for this book title and received immediate feedback! At the time of writing this book, there are 198 incredible consultants in that Slack channel. (Looking for someone to help you with grants, sponsorships, digital, graphic design, you name it—there's someone I know that can help!)

I decided, OK...this is amazing; this should exist for nonprofits to share ideas specifically around monthly giving programs!!

So, I didn't think twice when I decided to create The Sustainers, a Slack channel where any organization with a monthly giving program can join. Right from the beginning, the back-and-forth threads with ideas being shared have been INCREDIBLE.

If you want to join The Sustainers Slack Channel, scan the QR code here or go to positiveequation.com/book.

As I mentioned in the introduction, when you've turned the last page of this book, yes, you'll have a clear 5-Step Framework to build, grow, and sustain a successful recurring giving program. But, more than that, I hope it also leaves you with the confidence and clarity on how your mission can create sustainable revenue without the stress and pressure of constant fundraising.

Each chapter will outline a step in the framework with case studies, stories, tactical ideas, and guidance on how to get started. This book was designed to be your playground for brainstorming and creating lightbulb moments.

Please write all over this book, brainstorm, and create your own mastermind of peers!

To guide you, I've included "AHA Moments!" at the end of each chapter to highlight key takeaways and a brainstorming section called "Next Steps" for you to jot down your ideas.

Throughout these pages, we will explore practical steps and strategic insights to build and grow a successful monthly giving program. From understanding the historical context of recurring donations to leveraging modern technology and data, each chapter provides actionable advice to help nonprofits, aka YOU, thrive.

Just as it's so valuable to understand why a donor gave to you, before jumping into the tactical steps of the framework, it's important for me to share a bit about my story and why this all matters so deeply to me.

CHAPTER 2
My Story

I HAVEN'T BEEN in your *exact shoes*, but I've probably walked down similar roads throughout my career as a participant in the nonprofit sector from many different levels. I started as a donor, raising money in college for Knight-Thon, the University of Central Florida's Dance Marathon program supporting our local Children's Miracle Network hospitals. (*Shoutout to my fellow dancers that stood For The Kids! If you have nooo clue what I'm talking about, Google "dance marathons" and get ready to be blown away by some pretty epic photos,*) But it wasn't until I graduated and watched one movie that would forever change the projection of my life.

It was an average Friday night when a friend from college came to visit me in sunny Sarasota, Florida. We decided to keep things low-key and headed out to the nearest RedBox (hello 2011!) to rent a movie. When we got to the kiosk, we stood there, scrolling through titles debating about what to watch. After a few minutes of deliberation, we landed on a film called *The Whistleblower*.

We drove back to my apartment, and the smell of freshly popped popcorn filled the room as we settled in, poured two glasses of red, and snuggled into the couch. The film's intensity immediately gripped us, and soon, the outside world faded away, replaced by the stark and harrowing world portrayed on the screen.

A film we thought to be a fictional government thriller was actually the raw and unsettling portrayal of human trafficking—it was both eye-opening and gut-wrenching. I could feel my emotions churning as the protagonist uncovered layers of corruption and courageously fought against an overwhelming tide of injustice.

Then, as the movie drew to a close, the final credits began to roll, and those fateful words appeared on the screen: "Based on a True Story." I felt a jolt, like a bolt of lightning had struck me. It was as if the walls of my apartment had vanished, and I was suddenly thrust into the reality of the world outside, a world where these horrors were not just fiction but fact.

Curiosity and a sense of urgency drove me to research this true event. I discovered it was based on the true story of Kathryn Bolkovac, who uncovered a human trafficking scandal and corruption within the United Nations while working as a peacekeeper in Bosnia. Reading about her courageous efforts and the obstacles she faced was both inspiring and infuriating.

This was the first time I heard the term "human trafficking." I felt a mix of shock, disbelief, and a profound sense of injustice. How could something so horrific and widespread exist and I didn't know about it? The more I read, the deeper my outrage and determination grew. Kathryn Bolkovac's bravery and unwavering commitment to justice resonated with me on a deeply personal level.

Her story was a stark reminder of the power of one individual to make a difference, even in the face of overwhelming odds. I sat there, staring at the screen, my mind racing. Questions flooded my thoughts: How could this be happening? Why hadn't I known about it before? What could I do to make a difference? That night, a fire was ignited within me, a burning desire to contribute to a cause greater than myself. Little did I know, this would set me on a path that would profoundly shape my career and my life, leading me to dedicate myself to the nonprofit sector.

I started my first job out of college working for a small, local nonprofit, Take Stock in Children of Sarasota County (TSIC), as the Director of Development and Marketing. The position was both exhilarating and daunting, a perfect blend for a young professional eager to make a difference. Our mission was to provide college scholarships, mentorship, and hope to hundreds of students in need.

We were a spirited and scrappy group of four, united by our passion for the cause and determination to make a significant impact. The joy of seeing our efforts translate into real opportunities for the students was immensely gratifying. However, amid all this fulfillment, a part of me couldn't shake another dream. Deep down, I harbored a long-standing aspiration to live in New York City. So right in the heart of winter,

I made the move. Not sure what I was thinking about the seasonal timing...

The transition from then small-town Sarasota to the vibrant, fast-paced life of New York City was both exciting and overwhelming. My new neighborhood was a far cry from the quiet streets of Sarasota. Spanish Harlem was alive with culture and the constant hum of activity. I found myself both thrilled and intimidated by the sheer scale of the city.

In an effort to build a social network, I attended several NYC UCF Alumni events and watch parties, hoping to meet new friends and forge connections. It was at one of these events that a board member invited me to Hillsong Church. I decided to go, curious about what a church in New York City might be like.

Stepping into that church was unlike anything I had ever experienced before. The line of people waiting to enter stretched for blocks, creating an air of anticipation and excitement. The service was held at a concert venue with a bar in the back—this was definitely no traditional Presbyterian service that I attended growing up. The energy inside was contagious, the music powerful and soul-stirring.

I attended week after week, but one Sunday the sermon was delivered by a guest pastor, Christine Caine, co-founder of A21, an antitrafficking organization. Her words transported me right back to that moment in my Sarasota apartment when I first learned about human trafficking. A21's mission to reach, rescue, and restore lives across nineteen locations and fourteen countries struck a profound chord within me. I knew in that moment I had to be a part of it.

Eager to get involved, I participated in the A21 Freedom Walk in New York City. Alongside hundreds of others, we walked single file down 5th Avenue, holding posters with information about the realities of human trafficking. The experience was both sobering and empowering, a public declaration of solidarity and a call to action. I felt like I was part of something bigger than myself.

From there, I joined a Hillsong street team. Our mission was to visit strip clubs throughout the city, identify the house mom, and leave little bags with messages of hope, hair ties, and contact information in the back rooms. We wanted to reach out to the women working there, offering support and resources. Our group also met with survivors, listening to their stories of courage and resilience. I was in awe of their bravery and the strength it took to rebuild their lives.

The journey from a small-town girl in Florida to an active participant in New York City's fight against human trafficking was transformative. It was a journey that opened my eyes to the vastness of the world's problems and the incredible capacity for human resilience and hope. New York City, with all its challenges and opportunities, became not just a place to live but a place where I found my purpose and my voice.

It was through doing this mission work and reading one of my favorite books, *Good Is The New Cool* by Afdhel Aziz and Bobby Jones, that my life began to change. The book's powerful message about how businesses can do well by doing good resonated deeply with me, inspiring me to rethink my career and my contributions to the world.

At the time, I was working as a digital strategist at a public relations firm in the city. My days were filled with the fast-paced demands of city life, meetings, and RFP deadlines. Yet, as I sat at my desk, surrounded by a bustling office, I couldn't shake the feeling that something was missing. I longed for the sense of purpose and fulfillment that had driven me in my earlier work with nonprofits.

Driven by this craving for meaningful work, I decided to take action. I proposed the idea of launching a pro bono arm at the public relations firm. The premise was simple yet powerful: we would provide public relations and digital marketing services to a nonprofit for three months, focusing on a specific project. This initiative not only brought together different internal teams, fostering collaboration and camaraderie, but it also reignited my sense of purpose.

It was through doing pro bono projects that I had a pivotal realization: this was where I truly wanted to be. I wanted to leverage everything I had learned in the for-profit world—working on campaigns for Sports Illustrated, The Honest Company, The Weather Channel, and more—to help nonprofits tackle the world's biggest challenges.

Despite the risks and doubts swirling in my mind, I knew I had to follow my heart. In 2017, I took a leap of faith. I left behind my full-time digital marketing job and the familiar comfort of my life in New York City. I headed west to Los Angeles to start my own business—Positive Equation, a social media agency dedicated to nonprofits and social impact companies.

In the beginning, I took on traditional retainer work for various clients. From executing Movember's digital campaign in North America to creating social media assets for the LA84 Foundation and #HashtagLunchbag, and even managing digital sponsorship activations for the US Open and USTA's Net Generation Influencer program, I did it all. It was a whirlwind of projects that pushed me to expand my skills and adapt quickly.

From 2017 to 2019, I pivoted in my business more times than I can count trying to figure out the direction I wanted to take. I felt like a pinball, bouncing between various projects and ideas, always searching for that perfect fit.

Then in 2020, the world was in turmoil. The rising news of the pandemic and the Black Lives Matter movement gained global attention, highlighting issues of systemic racism, police brutality, and social injustice. It was a heavy, uncertain, and confusing time, and as a solopreneur, I was faced with yet another moment of reset. As nonprofits (and all businesses) went into crisis mode of how to navigate this completely digital world, I found myself questioning my decisions, feeling indecisive and completely alone as I navigated my business.

As the year was coming to an end, I heard a podcast episode where female entrepreneur business coach Julie Solomon talked about a mastermind program she would be leading in the new year. It was a year-long program where a small group of female entrepreneurs would be coached virtually each month and come together in-person twice. The concept of a mastermind, first introduced by Napoleon Hill in his book *Think and Grow Rich,* intrigued me.

In Napoleon Hill's words, a mastermind group is "the coordination of knowledge and effort of two or more people, who work toward a definite purpose, in the spirit of harmony." This principle is based on the belief that the synergy created by a group of motivated individuals can lead to extraordinary results.

Julie Solomon's mastermind program promised just that. Each month, we would have virtual coaching sessions where we could discuss our challenges, brainstorm solutions, and set actionable goals. The in-person retreats would offer an even deeper level of connection and collaboration, allowing us to build strong relationships and learn from each other's experiences face-to-face.

The idea of being part of such a dynamic group was both exciting and a little intimidating. I had never considered investing in myself or my business in this way, but I knew I needed something to get me out of my funk and connect with like-minded female entrepreneurs. After a five-figure investment (I was petrified to make), our mastermind calls began in January of 2021, and right away, my fear of what the heck did I just invest in vanished and turned into a complete release that I was exactly where I needed to be. I wasn't alone in my struggles. We were all facing similar challenges. It was during our first in-person trip to Nashville that I started to feel a shift within myself and my business.

In Napoleon Hill's words...

A MASTERMIND GROUP IS

"the coordination of knowledge and effort of two or more people, who work toward a **definite purpose,** in the **spirit of harmony."**

The energy and insights from the group were transformative! We shared our successes and failures, offered advice, and held each other accountable. The mastermind became a source of inspiration and motivation, pushing me to think bigger and take bolder steps in my business.

Being part of this mastermind not only helped me refine my business strategy but also gave me the confidence to pursue new opportunities and ideas. It was through this experience that I realized the value of community and the incredible impact that a supportive network can have on personal and professional growth.

The cumulative impact of all these experiences has led to this moment right now of writing this book.

As a donor, nonprofit employee, and now a consultant building monthly giving programs, I have certainly felt what you might be feeling.

It's OK to feel overwhelmed—*been there.*

It's OK to be scared about change or risk—*whew, REALLY been there.*

It's also OK to want to completely shake things up to see a different result!

Deep breaths…you got this!

Consider me your coach along the way to explore how to create and grow your monthly giving program.

Now, before we jump headfirst into the framework, it's important to get an understanding of how recurring giving fits into our economy and why it's received so much attention in recent years. That all begins by talking about the subscription economy.

CHAPTER 3
Subscriptions for Good

LET'S TRANSPORT BACK in time to the 1920s, a time when finding a good book wasn't as simple as a few clicks on your phone or computer. Back then, getting your hands on quality literature meant trips to the bookstore or library, both of which could be quite the hassle, especially if you lived in a rural area.

Enter the Book of the Month Club (BOMC), a revolutionary subscription idea by Harry Scherman, Maxwell Sackheim, and Robert Haas in 1926.

Harry Scherman envisioned a way to bring the best books directly to readers' homes. Together with Sackheim and Haas, he launched BOMC, offering subscribers a carefully selected book each month. This wasn't just any selection; it was curated by an esteemed editorial committee featuring literary giants.

Back in those days, BOMC was a game changer. In the first year, they acquired just 4,000 subscribers, but by 1927 the idea took off with 60,058!

The convenience and reliability of BOMC quickly resonated with American readers, reflecting a growing cultural shift.
This period marked a significant transformation in how people
consumed books, democratizing access to high-quality reads
and introducing many to new and diverse voices they might
not have discovered otherwise. By the '50s, they had 550,000
members, opening the eyes of many businesses to the power
of subscriptions.

BOMC was one of the earliest examples of
a subscription-based business. Who knew it would play such
a pivotal role in today's society?

So, why does this book and the discussion around recurring giving matter *right now*?

Taking a cue from the subscription economy
that's transformed how we shop and live, recurring giving has
become a core revenue stream in modern nonprofit fundraising.

In this chapter, we dive into the history of subscription
services and monthly donations, explore why smaller donation
amounts can be a big win, and break down the psychological
and strategic reasons behind recurring donations.

With a mix in expert insights, compelling stories, and
practical tips, you'll have a clear picture of why and how nonprofits—aka YOU—should focus on monthly giving programs.

THE SUBSCRIPTION ECONOMY

Here it is...the famous term "subscription economy." It might
sound pretty modern, and that's because it is! It came into the
spotlight in the early 21st century, largely thanks to the folks

over at a company called Zuora and its charismatic founder, Tien Tzuo. They started throwing around the term around 2010, and it really caught on. Tzuo was a big believer in changing how businesses think about making money. Instead of selling something once, why not have customers pay regularly? This way, businesses wouldn't just sell a product; they'd build ongoing relationships with their customers, ensuring a steady flow of income.

In his book, *Subscribed: Why the Subscription Model Will Be Your Company's Future—and What to Do About It,* Tien Tzuo reflects on the broader implications: "The way people buy has changed for good. We have new expectations as consumers. We prefer outcomes over ownership. We prefer customization, not standardization. And we want constant improvement, not planned obsolescence. We want a new way to engage with business. We want services, not products. The one-size-fits-all approach isn't going to cut it anymore. And to succeed in this new digital world, companies have to transform."

Like Tzuo mentions, this idea tapped into a bigger shift where people started preferring ongoing access to services and products rather than owning them outright—a trend boosted by the rise of the internet and digital technologies.

As evidenced by BOMC, the subscription model isn't a 21st-century invention. It's actually been around for centuries. For instance, take the publishing industry in the 17th century. Back then, books were sometimes sold via subscription; people would pay upfront before the book was even printed. This clever method let publishers gauge how many people were interested and gather funds for printing, all before the first page was set to ink. The idea goes even further back with maps and atlases in Europe during the 16th century, often sold on a subscription basis to fund explorations and costly print jobs.

The modern subscription economy, however, truly took off in the digital age. Companies like Netflix, founded in 1997, revolutionized the entertainment industry by offering a subscription-based streaming service in 2007. They are popularly known for being the king of widespread adoption.

Major technology companies like Adobe and Microsoft followed by transitioning from a large upfront enterprise cost to a lower recurring SaaS "software as a service" structure. The boom of subscription boxes took over in 2010 with the launch of the curated beauty box, Birchbox. Shortly after its launch, I was living in NYC and it seemed like every friend I spoke with had a Birchbox subscription to sample different beauty products each month.

Chewy, HelloFresh, Nuuly, Lovevery, FabFitFun, and many others hopped on the scene, and we haven't looked back since.

Starting to make a mental list of all your subscriptions? Yeah...start counting!

The numbers are also impressive—if you thought, like I did, this might be a nice trend, it doesn't show any signs of slowing down.

A recent Forbes article, "Subscription Service Model: How To Build A Profitable Business" by Cheryl Robinson, states the global subscription economy market size is projected to be $1.5 trillion in 2025, up from $650 billion in 2020. An average US consumer spent $273 monthly on subscription services in 2021 compared to $237 monthly in 2018.

The sentiment within the subscription industry also remains highly positive, with 96% of leaders expecting significant revenue growth.

And these companies don't mess around when it comes to the management of subscriptions.

Recurly, a company that specializes in subscription management, announced that in 2023 it successfully recovered over $1.2 billion in revenue for its clients that could have been lost due to payment issues. $1.2 billion!! This impressive recovery was made possible through their advanced technology and strategies designed to address and rectify payment failures, which is a common challenge.

The global subscription economy market size is projected to be $1.5 trillion in 2025, up from $650 billion in 2020. An average US consumer spent $273 monthly on subscription services in 2021 compared to $237 monthly in 2018.

As a nonprofit, you deal with this too.

Who are the donors that don't mean to "cancel" but do because their credit card expired? What percent of those people are part of your churn rate?

Retention and churn is paramount for a successful program, and businesses are paying attention.

GROWTH FROM THE INSIDE—FOCUS ON RETENTION & A SUSTAINER TEAM

According to a survey by Chargebee, 300+ industry leaders from the biggest subscription companies are shifting their focus from just acquiring new customers to maximizing revenue from their existing ones. They're all talking about their game plan for 2024, and there's a buzzword on everyone's lips— retention. It's also a strategic pivot that holds immense value for nonprofits, especially when it comes to recurring giving.

Now, let's zoom in on this crucial point.

In the nonprofit world, there's often an obsession with outward growth. The drive to secure new donors is relentless, while the potential goldmine of existing, smaller donors can be overlooked. Think about it: many nonprofits have a Major Gifts Officer on payroll, someone dedicated to chasing those big, one-time donations. But how often do you see a Sustainer Role, a person focused solely on nurturing and growing recurring, smaller gifts? It's rare, and that's a missed opportunity.

The data from the Chargebee survey highlights a lesson the nonprofit sector can learn from the subscription economy: the power of retention and recurring support. In the for-profit world, this translates to steady revenue and long-term customer loyalty. For nonprofits, it means sustainable funding, predictable income streams, and a more engaged donor base.

Imagine hiring a team specifically to support the growth of recurring giving programs. These are professionals who would focus on making monthly donors feel valued and appreciated, much like how BOMC curated and nurtured their subscriber base. This team would employ strategies to retain these donors, ensuring they feel connected to the cause and see the impact of their contributions regularly.

Investing in such a team isn't just a good idea—it's essential.

These roles could include a Sustainer Program Manager, responsible for designing and implementing engagement strategies, and a Donor Relations Specialist, who ensures every recurring donor feels like a valued part of the nonprofit's mission.

The result?

Increased donor retention, higher lifetime value of donors, and a more stable financial foundation for the nonprofit.

Just as we saw with BOMC's editorial committee—they were crucial in selecting books that kept subscribers excited and engaged—a dedicated team for sustaining giving would be vital in keeping donors connected and committed. This approach fosters a culture of gratitude and recognition, ensuring that small, consistent gifts are not just an afterthought but a cornerstone of the nonprofit's funding strategy.

While the nonprofit sector often celebrates the big wins with major gifts, it's time to shine a spotlight on the humble, consistent contributions that, over time, can build a robust and resilient organization.

Investing in such a team isn't just a good idea— **it's essential.**

Hiring a team to support the growth of recurring giving is not just about managing donations—it's about building relationships, fostering loyalty, and ensuring long-term sustainability.

EXAMPLES OF FOR-PROFIT SUBSCRIPTION BUSINESSES

I wanted to call out a few examples of companies that see the important business benefits of recurring customers but also do a great job of marketing. I recommend taking a peek and see what stands out to you.

Usually, the top subscriptions that come to mind are entertainment based, but there's been a new wave of subscriptions that do good in recent years too. Each of these companies highlight a prime example of a step in the 5-Step Framework that we'll review in the upcoming chapters.

Let's take a look…

1. **Who Gives A Crap**—This toilet paper subscription service donates 50% of its profits to help build toilets and improve sanitation in the developing world. The copy on their website is gold:

    "Who knew changing the world could be as easy as changing your toilet paper? (Ok, we did.)

    We believe we can make the world a better place when we work together. Sure, over 1 million trees are destroyed every day just to make regular toilet paper. Giant corporations pump out poorly made junk that no one needs. And billions of people lack access to clean water or a toilet. It's crappy, but we know we have the power to make a change. We just need your help."

2. **Thrive Market**—An organic online grocery platform that wants to make living healthy a priority and accessible to everyone. They offer a membership-based service where, for every paid membership, a free membership is provided to a low-income family, student, teacher, veteran, or first responder.

   With one million Instagram followers, they're a great example of an organization that showcases the value of what they provide, capturing the attention of potential new members. As a new mom, I've been targeted constantly with their advertising.

3. **Winc**—A wine subscription company that focuses on sustainable and organic wine production, aiming to reduce the environmental impact of winemaking.

   If you visit their Instagram account, the content is full of memes and cultural references speaking right to their target demographic.

4. **Imperfect Foods**—They deliver subscription boxes of "ugly" fruits and vegetables that might otherwise go to waste, helping to reduce food waste.

   Immediately on their website, they're calling in the people they want with a graphic that says, "For Thoughtful Eaters." If that's not you, you might click out. But, if that is you, the intrigue continues with the ability to start your subscription for free.

So creative, right!? One glance on each of these websites and you know immediately who they're trying to attract.

Is the reason why we're so quick to pull out our wallets for these services similar to what drives us to give? Let's explore.

WHY DO DONORS GIVE RECURRING VS. ONE-TIME?

For donors, there are several psychological and practical factors. We'll review the application of these factors more in Chapter 7, Step 2: Make It Easy, but it's important to look at a high level first to assess the overall temperature of how and why people give.

1. **Consistency and Habit Formation:** People are more likely to stick with actions that become habitual. Recurring donations create a routine, making it easier for donors to continue their support over time.

2. **Emotional Engagement:** People give in memory or honor of their loved ones. Regular donations reinforce a donor's emotional connection to a cause. By contributing consistently, donors feel more invested in the organization's mission and progress.

   Zooming in on emotional engagement, based on the 111,514 recurring gifts in the 2024 Neon One Recurring Giving Report, approximately 13,000 included notes from donors. These notes are incredibly powerful to better understand the reason behind why people give.

THE TOP 5 SENTIMENTS WERE:

1. **Gratitude**—Thankful for the nonprofit's work. Quite a few of the supporters noted they were direct beneficiaries.
2. **Love**—For donors' loved ones or love for the organization.
3. **Honor**—Honoring individuals, the organization's services, or memories.
4. **Inspiration**—Inspired by the work of the nonprofit or a staff member.
5. **Remembrance**—Left in memory of a loved one.

3. **Perceived Impact:** Recurring donations allow donors to see the long-term impact of their contributions. This sustained engagement can lead to a greater sense of satisfaction and fulfillment.

4. **Budget Management:** Smaller, recurring donations are often easier to manage within a donor's budget compared to larger, one-time gifts. This approach makes philanthropy more accessible and sustainable for a wider audience.

And what I believe to be the most important...

5. **Expression of Values & Personal Identity:** When people donate to causes they care about, it's more than just a financial transaction—it's a way to express and reinforce their personal values and beliefs. This kind of giving helps align their actions with what they stand for, which strengthens their sense of self. According to "Altruism and the Self" by Gneezy, altruistic behavior, including charitable donations, is strongly tied to self-perception and the desire to maintain a positive self-image.

Donating creates a sense of belonging.

Just like my march with A21, when you contribute to a cause, you become part of a community of like-minded individuals, which can make you feel connected and valued. It's a bit like joining a club where everyone shares the same mission. Overall, giving helps people see themselves as good and moral. This boost in moral self-image is great for self-esteem. Donors often feel proud and gain a sense of self-worth from their contributions. It's like getting a gold star for doing something meaningful. "The Psychology of Giving," a study by Dunn, Aknin, and Norton (2008), found that spending money on others leads to greater happiness compared to spending it on oneself, highlighting the emotional rewards of giving.

On top of that, donating triggers some serious feel-good vibes.

In the 2006 study by Jorge Moll and colleagues, "The Neuroscience of Giving," they found that giving activates the mesolimbic pathway in the brain, which is the reward

DONATING creates a sense of *Belonging*

center, leading to feelings of happiness and satisfaction. This psychological reward can create a fulfilling sense of purpose and encourage continued giving. For some, public recognition, like being listed as a donor or receiving a thank-you note, enhances their self-esteem and reaffirms their identity as generous individuals. Even without public acknowledgment, knowing that their donation made a difference can still boost their positive self-view.

As you start thinking about your own community of recurring supporters and their personal motivations, I decided to poll a few of my colleagues paving the way when it comes to the technology advancements and strategies for regular giving.

HERE'S WHAT THEY HAD TO SAY:

Soraya Alexander

President of Classy and COO of GoFundMe

Why do you give monthly?

My one-time gifts are often in response to a momentary call to attention or in response to a single compelling ask. On the other hand, I tend to give monthly to declare my enduring commitment to a particular organization. My recurring gifts have little to do with dollars and more to do with a signal of sustained participation in an organization and its mission. It feels more participatory and reflects more enduring elements of my self-identity.

What trends do you see when it comes to recurring giving?

Successful subscription-based companies go beyond mere transactions, using subscriptions to deepen customer engagement and loyalty. Rather than a simple 'set it and forget it' model, these companies recognize that subscribers are invested in their brand, seeking an ongoing relationship and using this participation as a way to deepen their relationship with these consumers. For instance, Disney+ doesn't just offer content; it connects users to the entire Disney experience, including memorable Disney Parks visits. Similarly, recurring gifts highlight for nonprofits where their most dedicated supporters are—regardless of capacity to give. Recurring donors are the most concentrated cohort of donors who are signaling that they want to be further activated on behalf of your organization. This is your invitation to draw them in further.

The most powerful recurring programs live in the organizations that get creative—both in how to engage this group and also in how to invite them to become more active participants in advancing the cause. One of my favorite examples of this is Broadway Cares, which has created a "NextGen Network" of young professionals who make an annual contribution of $250 or more on a recurring basis. They use this opportunity to not only treat this group to exclusive invitations but also give these individuals ways to connect and engage with each other around the commonality that they are younger donors who actively participate in the same meaningful cause.

According to Classy's platform data, recurring donors are nine times more valuable than one-time donors, and the average expected lifetime of a recurring donation is 4.6 years.

Due to this strength, nonprofit customers that focus most heavily on cultivating their recurring donor bases see up to two-thirds of their entire online donation volume coming from recurring contributions. Of first-time donors who go on to establish a sustaining gift, they see one-third of them do so in the first ninety days. Communicate early and often with the impact and the ask.

Max Friedman

Co-Founder, Givebutter

Why do you give monthly?

People! At the heart of every monthly gift are people who make my gift matter. I love getting asked to support monthly because it sparks a conversation around the sustainability of my gift and the impact it will make over longer periods of time.

What trends do you see when it comes to recurring giving?

Givebutter has seen significant growth in recurring donations over the past few years. As of 2024, 7,085 organizations are receiving recurring donations on the platform. This represents a substantial increase, with a 112% year-over-year rise in organizations benefiting from recurring gifts. When comparing individual versus recurring donations, there has been a noticeable shift towards recurring donations. In January 2024, 12% of all donations were recurring. To put this in perspective, recurring donations have doubled in four years, increasing from 6% in January 2021 to 12% in January 2024.

The progression has been steady: 6% in 2021, 8% in 2022, 11% in 2023, and 12% in 2024. The average recurring donation amount is $67.32 per month, equalling over $800 per year.

When considering all recurring frequencies, such as weekly or annually, the average increases to $83.58. This data underscores the growing importance and impact of recurring donations for nonprofits using the Givebutter platform.

Abigail Jarvis

Head of Content, Neon One

Why do you give monthly?

When I look at the nonprofits I support on a monthly basis, the common denominator is that they're all aligned with my hobbies and interests. The most recent monthly gift I set up was to The Chattooga Conservancy, an organization that works to protect an area where I grew up camping and backpacking. I love it there and I recently spent some time camping up there. Setting up a monthly gift was one of the first things I did when I got home.

What trends do you see when it comes to recurring giving?

The rising popularity of monthly subscriptions is really remarkable, and I think it's making people more open to the idea of setting up monthly donations.

We found some really encouraging trends around recurring giving. Between 2018 and 2022, the average nonprofit's base of recurring donors grew 127% even though most of them saw a slight decline in total active supporters. Those people represented an increasingly large percentage of total donors, which means that segment of supporters is growing more quickly than others.

When it comes to the number of individual gifts vs. recurring gifts—the number of recurring gifts is going up! Between 2018 and 2022, the average total number of all donations to a nonprofit—including recurring ones—rose around 2.25%. When we looked at the total number of recurring gifts only, we found that they increased 144%. That's huge!

What's even more exciting is that recurring gifts represented an increasingly large percentage of nonprofits' total revenue. In 2018, that kind of gift represented less than 1% of the average nonprofit's revenue. By 2022, that had risen to more than 2%. That might not sound huge at first, but it's a really encouraging sign. In 2022, the average monthly gift was $78.43.

It's important, though, not to equate a monthly gift to a beloved cause with something transactional, like a Netflix subscription. It's compassion, not consumerism! Keeping that difference in mind is absolutely critical.

Salvatore Salpietro

Chief Community Officer, Fundraise Up

Why do you give monthly?

It has to be a cause that I'm connected to and that resonates with me. The more specific that my gift will be applied, not necessarily unrestricted funds versus restricted funds, but if I know that this is going to be used to help animals in abusive situations or will be used to feed children in a specific situation, the clearer that's conveyed to me, the more I can visualize the impact that my gift will have. That's one thing.

The second two are kind of subtle and passive. If the website doesn't look professional, I lose trust that they'll be able to use my money efficiently. If the donation form or experience is antiquated or looks dated, I'm not going to trust putting my data into that and layering on that I'm typically looking at my personal emails on my phone when I'm on the couch, when I'm at the park with my daughter, whatever it might be, and I'm not pulling out my credit card. I'm not typing in a bunch of information. If you've got Apple Pay, if you've got PayPal, if you've got something that I can give without thinking too hard or doing too much, I'm way more likely to make a gift.

What trends do you see when it comes to recurring giving?

Fundraise Up has nearly 3,000 nonprofits using its platform, and pretty much all of them are accepting recurring donations. Most nonprofits on modern platforms see an increase in monthly donations when implemented correctly with the right strategy. The average monthly gift on Fundraise Up is around $37.80, which increases to $42.80 for desktop users and slightly decreases to $37.50 for mobile users. More than half of donations are made via mobile devices, indicating significant mobile engagement.

The trend towards recurring donations is expected to continue as donors' expectations align with consumer behavior in other contexts. Despite a 1% decline in the ratio of recurring plans in 2023 compared to 2022, the average donation amount increased by 8.5%, which offsets the decline. Additionally, about 3%-5% of donors convert from one-time to monthly when asked.

I ALSO REACHED OUT TO FELLOW NONPROFIT CONSULTANTS AND SOME OF MY DEAR FRIENDS IN THIS SPACE TO ASK THEM WHY THEY ELECT TO GIVE MONTHLY.

Here are their thoughts:

One of the most stylish and profound keynote speakers that's an expert on leadership, Kishshana Palmer said, I give monthly to organizations that I care deeply about their issue area. And either I know that vitality and sustainability is something that the organization really struggles with, and so having a consistent stream of revenue coming in is going to be really important. I will stop giving to an organization monthly if I don't get at least an annual acknowledgment that I'm a monthly giver. I don't need to get all the stories. I don't need to get all the stuff, but I do want to see if there's a specific call-out for donors like me who give monthly and acknowledgement that that really helps with the operations of the organization so that they can activate, accelerate, and amplify the mission.

Host of What the Fundraising and creator of Power Partners™, Mallory Erickson shares her stance on giving monthly: Being in the field and knowing how fundraisers perceive monthly giving and the stability it creates, I focus my monthly giving on issues in organizations that I know I want to be involved in for a long time and I don't want to forget to give to them during a particular time of the year. I want them to know that they can count on me and that I am really in this with them and will be month after month. I would say the organizations I donate to monthly are those that are the most core to my identity, values, and my hopes and dreams for the work!

When looking for a perspective driven by data, I always turn to Chief Data Officer at Giving Tuesday, Woodrow Rosenbaum. He shared, "Research is showing that people engage in recurring giving because of a deep personal and emotional connection to a cause. Those donors are more valuable over time, and they are retained at higher levels. We've also seen that recurring giving is particularly popular with younger donors. Because of those patterns, I think there is substantial untapped opportunity for monthly giving that can make nonprofits more resilient and help cement closer, longer-term relationships with supporters."

One of the kindest souls I know, an epic storyteller and cohost of the podcast *We Are For Good*, Becky Endicott told me, Monthly giving is about sustainability + experience + shared community. When I choose to give monthly to an org, I first look for value alignment. Do we believe and fight for the same things? If so, I want to be a rabid fan of your mission. Second, I choose causes wrapped around my identity and the change I want to see in the world—women's empowerment, social justice, climate change, literacy, arts, and poverty.

I come for the mission, but I stay for the community. I want to follow these missions. I want to be educated by them. I want to celebrate them alongside my fellow rabid fans. And I want to activate on their behalf. And I want the organization to know I am highly invested in what they're doing and they can count on me for sustainable funding + activating into the solution. I invest in places where I feel my one modest gift fuels a bigger collective pushing toward immediate solutions. Big dreamers, innovators, and visionaries who can back up their work with data and stories from the front line attract me.

To summarize these incredible people and why they choose to give regularly:

1. **Enduring Commitment:** Monthly donations reflect a deep, sustained commitment to an organization, signaling ongoing participation and aligning with one's self-identity.

2. **Sustainability and Impact:** Monthly giving fosters conversations about the long-term impact and sustainability of donations, emphasizing the human connection behind each gift.

3. **Recognition and Consistency:** Consistent recognition of monthly donors, noting that acknowledgment of their contributions enhances their ongoing support and connection to the organization's mission. What my peers shared directly correlates to the studies discussed above. Being sent routine impactful communication reaffirms their initial decision to give and fills their personal identity.

4. **Trust and Ease of Giving:** The importance of a professional, user-friendly donation experience. Trust in the organization's ability to use funds efficiently and the ease of making a donation (e.g., via Apple Pay or PayPal) significantly influence their decision to give regularly.

When the ask to give is made, it's important to take all of these things into account. What are the most common reasons you hear that people give to your organization?

Jot them down here!

_____

_____

_____

_____

_____

_____

_____

_____

WHEN WAS THE FIRST MONTHLY DONATION?

It's an interesting question.

The concept of regular giving can be traced back centuries, with roots in religious and charitable practices. However, the formalization of monthly donations in the nonprofit sector began more recently. In the early 20th century, organizations like the Red Cross and the Salvation Army started implementing structured fundraising campaigns that included recurring donations. These efforts aimed to provide a steady flow of resources to support ongoing humanitarian efforts.

A notable example is the National Society for the Prevention of Cruelty to Children (NSPCC) in the UK, which pioneered regular giving in the 1980s. Their Sponsor a Child program allowed donors to contribute a fixed amount each month, directly supporting individual children in need. This model proved highly successful and inspired many other nonprofits to adopt similar approaches.

Over the last decade, the rise of the subscription economy has reshaped not just business landscapes but also charitable giving. As more consumers become accustomed to the convenience and continuity of subscriptions for everyday services, the trend is strongly mirrored in the nonprofit sector through the growth of monthly giving programs.

The shift from one-time donations to monthly gifts is significant, not just for its financial predictability but for the sustained engagement it offers between donors and charities.

Data underscore this shift.

The 2024 Neon One Recurring Giving Report references donor data from 2018 to 2022 and provides fascinating findings:

- The average nonprofit grew its recurring donor base by 127%!
- Average recurring retention rate of 78%, significantly higher than that of one-time donors, which most publications say hovers around 60%. From my personal conversations, I see the one-time retention rate even lower, around 40%.
- In 2022, the average nonrecurring donor supported a nonprofit for about 1.68 years. In contrast, during the same year, the average lifetime of a recurring donor was 7.71 years!
- 50% of recurring donors give additional gifts…begs the question, are you asking?

The significant move towards recurring donations has been facilitated by advances in technology, making it easier for donors to set up and manage their contributions online.

Monthly giving programs are now the cornerstone of stability for many nonprofits with their funding and impact.

CONVINCED IT'S A WORTHWHILE INVESTMENT?

You bought this book, so I'm leaning towards yes...but along this journey of building, scaling, and sustaining your recurring giving supporters, I don't want to sugarcoat it: you'll likely encounter moments where it just feels HARD.

No one is joining.
You sent out an email and heard crickets back.
There's just not enough time in the day to get it all done.
I hear you.

To push through these challenges, it's important to approach each hurdle with a growth mindset. And to share what I mean, let me introduce you to one of my favorite podcasts, *Business Wars*.

AHA Moments!

1. **Recurring Donations—The Backbone of Modern Non-profits:** Fast forward to today, and recurring giving is a cornerstone of nonprofit fundraising. Monthly giving programs provide nonprofits with a stable, predictable revenue stream. This consistency allows for better planning, budgeting, and long-term project sustainability. Nonprofits that embrace this model can navigate financial uncertainties with more confidence, ensuring their mission continues without interruption.

2. **Increased Donor Lifetime Value:** Monthly donors often contribute more over time compared to one-time donors. For instance, a $20 monthly donation amounts to $240 annually, which is often more than a one-time gift. This sustained giving builds stronger relationships between donors and nonprofits, leading to higher donor retention rates and increased lifetime value. Data shows that the average lifetime of a recurring donor is significantly longer than that of a one-time donor, with recurring donors supporting nonprofits for about 7.71 years on average compared to 1.68 years for nonrecurring donors.

3. **Psychological and Practical Benefits:** The psychological impact of recurring donations cannot be overstated. Monthly giving aligns with modern financial habits, offering

a low-friction, high-continuity experience. Donors feel more emotionally connected to the cause, seeing their contributions as part of a larger, ongoing impact. This emotional engagement, coupled with the practical ease of smaller, manageable monthly contributions, makes recurring giving a preferred choice for many supporters.

4. **The Subscription Economy—Lessons for Nonprofits:** The subscription economy, popularized by companies like Netflix and Zuora, emphasizes the value of ongoing relationships over one-time transactions. Nonprofits can learn from this model by focusing on donor retention and sustained engagement. By creating a sense of community and continuous impact, nonprofits can build a loyal base of supporters who see their monthly contributions as integral to the organization's mission. This shift from one-time donations to recurring gifts mirrors the broader trend in consumer behavior towards subscription-based services, highlighting the relevance and necessity of monthly giving programs in today's world.

NEXT STEPS:

_____

_____

_____

_____

_____

_____

_____

CHAPTER 4
Growth Mindset

BUSINESS WARS IS a podcast produced by Wondery that delves into the intense and often cutthroat competition between well-known companies. Each season of the podcast explores a different rivalry, revealing the behind-the-scenes stories and strategies that shape how we live and what we buy. The show is hosted by David Brown and provides listeners with an in-depth look at the corporate battles that influence our world. Highly recommend you check it out for any upcoming road trips!

The "Netflix vs. Blockbuster" season was the very first season of *Business Wars*, premiering on February 6, 2018. This season explores the fierce competition between Netflix and Blockbuster, highlighting the technological innovations, business strategies, and critical decisions that ultimately led to Netflix's rise and Blockbuster's downfall.

Revisit the past with me again.

It's the early 2000s, and Blockbuster is the king of the video rental world, with stores on every corner and a loyal customer base addicted to those Friday night movie binges. Who doesn't remember the phrase, "Be kind, please rewind."

Enter Netflix, a scrappy startup offering DVDs by mail, no late fees, and eventually, the radical concept of streaming movies online. Blockbuster chuckled at this fledgling competitor, even passing up the chance to buy Netflix for a mere $50 million. Big mistake.

As Netflix invested in technology, embraced data, and transitioned to streaming, Blockbuster clung to its physical stores, burdened by debt and a refusal to innovate. By the time Blockbuster launched its own online rental service, Netflix had already moved on, conquering the digital frontier and making late fees a thing of the past.

Blockbuster's failure was a classic tale of resting on laurels and resisting change, while Netflix's rise was a masterclass in forward-thinking, adaptability, and seizing the digital age by the horns.

So, what's the moral of the story?

When it comes to monthly giving programs, don't be a Blockbuster.

Look ahead, embrace innovation, and invest in a subscription for good. A robust monthly giving program is your organization's Netflix moment—a chance to build a sustainable future, engage supporters continuously, and create lasting impact. Because in the ever-evolving world of philanthropy, staying ahead of the curve is the only way to ensure you're not left behind.

Sometimes it's hard to realize that we're falling behind and when it's time to adapt and innovate when we're SO close to our own work.

IMPORTANCE OF ADAPTATION

To highlight the importance of adaptation in business, let's look at another two familiar companies—Kodak and Apple—with vastly different outcomes based on their approach to change, their why, and their structure.

Kodak was once a powerhouse in the photography industry, dominating the market with its film products. What's wild is despite inventing the first digital camera in 1975, Kodak continued to prioritize its traditional film business. Astonishingly, just a year later, Kodak commanded 90% of film sales and 85% of camera sales in the U.S., according to a 2005 case study for Harvard Business School. In 1996, Kodak was the fifth most valuable brand in the world.

However, Kodak's hesitation to fully embrace digital technology, despite its early innovations, led to its downfall. As digital photography surged forward, Kodak clung to its film business, missing critical opportunities to lead in the digital market. The company's reluctance to pivot and adapt to the changing technological landscape proved costly. By the early 2000s, Kodak began to struggle financially as digital cameras became more popular. Despite efforts to catch up, the company could not regain its former dominance. Kodak's filing for bankruptcy in 2012, marked a significant chapter in the

Look ahead, embrace innovation, and **invest in a subscription for good.**

company's decline from industry leader to a cautionary tale of missed opportunities and resistance to change.

Today Kodak has emerged from bankruptcy and, while no longer a giant in the photography world, is finding a new path by leveraging its expertise in imaging technology to serve different markets.

Kodak's reluctance to innovate is a classic example of what happens when a company fails to adapt to changing times. They were heavily invested in their traditional film products and didn't see the potential of digital photography until it was too late. Competitors like Canon and Nikon capitalized on this opportunity, leading the market while Kodak lagged behind.

In comparison, Apple has consistently reinvented itself by embracing innovation and change. As we've seen with every movie about Steve Jobs, they started as a computer company, but Apple evolved over time as culture and society demanded. They expanded into the music industry with the iPod, revolutionized the phone industry with the iPhone, and transformed how we consume media with the iPad and now entertainment with Apple TV.

Apple's willingness to take risks, embrace innovation, and constantly push the boundaries has made it one of the most successful companies in the world.

They didn't let fear of change hold them back; they used it as a catalyst for growth.

We see this happen time and time again with nonprofits as well. Several organizations have struggled to remain operational due to the inability to adapt to changing circumstances. Let's take a look at a few examples.

San Diego Opera: In 2014, the San Diego Opera announced its closure due to financial insolvency. The organization struggled with declining attendance and revenue, compounded by a failure to innovate in its programming and marketing strategies. Although the opera eventually avoided shutting down through community efforts and restructuring, its near collapse was a stark example of the risks of not innovating. What avoided the shutdown? Community efforts and a focus on restructuring. Great example of not waiting until it's too late to think about doing things differently.

Let's take a look at another organization that wasn't able to survive due to lack of updated fundraising methods.

Hull House: This 123-year-old historic social services organization in Chicago, cofounded by Jane Addams (the first American woman to receive the Nobel Peace Prize) in 1889, filed for bankruptcy in 2012. Hull House's financial troubles were attributed to its failure to modernize fundraising efforts and adapt to new social service delivery models, leading to a significant decrease in funding and operational viability. Over time, the organization became heavily reliant on government revenue, and when public spending cuts occurred, private donations weren't sufficient to fill the gap.

What's particularly interesting about Hull House is that before the charitable tax deduction took effect in 1917, it was entirely funded by private gifts, with no tax benefit to donors. Initially, individual gifts fully supported the initiative, but over time, the organization shifted to depend more on government dollars, ultimately contributing to its financial downfall.

The rise of the subscription economy was well underway. But these organizations didn't have the foresight or awareness to dial in on a potential solution with creating a strong recurring giving program. Not to say that if these organizations had recurring donor programs they wouldn't have faced challenges, but it's a steady stream that provides more predictable funding from a mass group of people instead of heavily relying on a select few major donors or large grants.

Remember the fifteen organizations I interviewed for this book? I asked them all:

"If you could go back in time, what would you have done differently?"

Can you guess what nearly every organization said?

Start sooner.

Whether you have a full team and marketing budget ready to go, or you're a team of one that realizes recurring giving is essential to sustain your efforts—just start.

If I waited for the "perfect moment" to know what I was doing when starting Positive Equation, I never would have taken the leap.

If it seems like I'm *continually* emphasizing the importance of recurring giving models, it's because I truly believe they are vital to the health of the nonprofit sector. Yet, when it comes to prioritizing recurring giving, we often pause, question, and get nervous to prioritize it.

Embrace the belief that you are offering someone the greatest gift: the opportunity to have a deeper purpose by supporting a cause that resonates deeply with who they are.

As you read this book, my suggestion is to stay curious and open to new ideas. I catch myself sometimes going, "No way, I could never…" before I even allow the thought a chance to take shape.

Cassandra Worthy, a renowned speaker and expert on change management, has shared numerous insights on growth through change. She advises that organizations should not just survive through disruptions but use them as a catalyst for growth.

This involves cultivating a growth mindset and seeing every change as a moment of opportunity rather than a threat. In her book *Change Enthusiasm: How to Harness the Power of Emotion for Leadership and Success* she shares, "When disruption rocks your world, whether it be a challenging relationship with a new manager, an organizational restructure, an acquisition, or a job loss, once you've accepted your invitation into the opportunity presented, trust that the opportunity to grow is boundless."

These words echo a crucial theme for this book: the importance of a growth mindset in expanding and nurturing a successful monthly giving program.

Embracing Change

...and viewing it as an opportunity rather than a threat can **transform how non-profits operate,** innovate, and engage with their supporters.

Embracing change and viewing it as an opportunity rather than a threat can transform how nonprofits operate, innovate, and engage with their supporters.

A growth mindset encourages curiosity and the exploration of "what if" scenarios.

For you, this means continually asking questions and seeking new ways to engage donors:

➔ What if we offered exclusive content to our monthly donors?
➔ What if we created a community platform for them to share their stories and connect with one another?
➔ What if we personalized our communication to reflect each donor's unique journey with our organization?

These questions open the door to innovative strategies that can enhance donor engagement and retention. By fostering a culture of curiosity, nonprofits can discover untapped potential and create meaningful experiences for their supporters.

As we delve into the chapters ahead, let's keep Cassandra Worthy's wisdom at the forefront: embrace change, cultivate curiosity, and harness emotional power to fuel growth. With this mindset, you can build a robust and resilient monthly giving program that not only sustains your mission but also creates lasting, meaningful connections with your supporters.

Let's put this all into practice and dive into the 5-Step Framework to build, grow, and sustain a subscription for good!

BUILD
GROW
SUSTAIN
BUILD
GROW
SUSTAIN
BUILD
GROW

PART TWO

BUILD
GROW
SUSTAIN
BUILD
GROW
SUSTAIN
BUILD
GROW

CHAPTER 5

The 5-Step Framework to Build, Grow, & Sustain Subscriptions for Good

IN THE SUSTAINERS Slack Group[2] a comment was posted: "Is there somewhere or something that I can read to get an overview on how to set up and manage a robust recurring donor program?"

Let me take you on a journey through a proven framework that's been crafted from years of experience, industry insights, and a deep dive into what truly works in the world of monthly giving programs. Drawing from my background in digital marketing, countless conversations with nonprofit professionals, and the creation of over fifteen monthly giving programs, I've distilled this into a clear, actionable guide of five steps.

You might have seen plenty of general advice online about setting up a monthly giving program, but what really makes one thrive?

That's exactly what you're about to uncover.

---

2   A slack channel connecting nonprofits focused growing monthly giving programs. Learn more at positiveequation.com/book.

As we walk through each step of this framework, I'll share real stories and examples to show you how these principles come to life.

THE 5-STEP FRAMEWORK TO BUILD, GROW, & SUSTAIN A SUBSCRIPTION FOR GOOD:

Step 1: Create the Product

First, let's dive into the "why" and structure behind your program. What makes it special? We'll look at how to structure it effectively and build a brand that resonates. This is where you lay the foundation, creating something compelling that donors can connect with.

Step 2: Make It Easy

Next, it's all about giving your program a homebase, aka a web page. We'll explore the outline of a monthly giving landing page and ways to optimize the donation experience, ensuring it's seamless and user-friendly. Remember, the easier you make it for people to give and manage their ongoing gift, the more likely they are to commit.

Step 3: Call in the Believers

Who are the champions of your cause? We'll identify the right language, partners, and activations that inspire people to take action. This step is about rallying a community of believers who are passionate about your mission.

Step 4: Make the Ask

Here's where we go all-in with marketing and promotion to ask for recurring gifts! You'll hear from five organizations on how they've asked supporters to grow their communities, promotional ideas, and answers to top FAQs.

Step 5: Remind with Joy + Gratitude

Finally, you'll start to define a twelve-month (and beyond) retention strategy that works for you. This step is about reminding your donors of their incredible impact and expressing gratitude in meaningful ways. Keeping the joy of giving alive ensures long-term commitment and support.

Think of your monthly giving program as a tool to harness the passion of your supporters. There are already die-hard fans out there talking about your work.

Your job is to call them in and nurture that community.

As you explore each step of this framework, you'll find actionable insights and inspiring examples that bring these concepts to life. Let's embark on this journey together and transform how your organization engages with its supporters, creating a sustainable future built on recurring generosity!

CHAPTER 6
Step 1: Create the Product

WHEN WAS THE last time you made a purchase?

If you're like me, probably ten minutes ago on Amazon or during your weekly Target run that was meant for one thing but turned into...well... a whole lot more than one thing! Whether you were online or shopping in a store, you purchased a product that likely involved a whole team deeply discussing the market analysis, why it has to be THIS color, that name, the exact price it needed to be, where and how it would be marketed, and all the other hundreds of decisions that come together when creating a product that will be delivered into the hands of consumers.

Now, with ALL that said, if you try to get every single detail "perfect," nothing would ever launch, right? The beautiful thing about the product you're creating is it's editable. You can always update a name, change the website, rewrite copy, etc. Throughout this book, you'll learn the important elements to include and then iterate as culture, your mission, and time pass on.

In this chapter, you'll learn how to conceptualize and build your monthly giving program as a unique product that resonates with your supporters. We'll cover the importance of understanding the why and impact behind your program, and the critical steps to naming and branding your initiative. By thinking of your program as a product, you'll be equipped to develop a compelling offering that not only attracts but also retains loyal donors. This chapter will provide you with practical exercises, real-life examples, and actionable insights to kickstart your monthly giving program with a strong foundation.

Throughout this book, you might come across some ideas that make you pause and think, "Umm…you want me to try what?!" These are what I like to call "Mindset Shifts."

Let's kick things off with the first one.

MINDSET SHIFT: I want you to think of your monthly giving program as a unique product that you're offering to supporters. Just like any new product—whether you buy a pair of shoes or a car—it needs a solid marketing strategy, a dedicated budget, and a passionate team to promote it. The mindframe I want you to try and instill is that your monthly giving program is a product—not just a checkbox on a donation form.

And to successfully promote a product there needs to be a full team effort that it's a priority, or if you're a team of one—your priority. It's receiving dedicated time and financial support.

So, whether you're a team of one or hundreds, what's the personnel, marketing, technology, and tools, that it will take to run this product?

It's time to dive into that annual budget and look at how you can allocate funds to this new offer you'll have.

I recently had a conversation with a nonprofit organization, and they shared that to elevate their program to the next level, they recognize the need to increase their investment in marketing and the technology that will support their growth.

Stepping into the next level of growth and creating this product can be scary, no doubt!

Someone I look up to as a business mentor is Marie Forleo. In her book *Everything is Figureoutable* she shares, "Everything you've ever wanted is sitting on the other side of fear." She encourages embracing fear as a sign that you are on the right path.

There's often fear associated with recurring giving at the beginning because it's not an event or one-off campaign where a bulk of funds will come in all at once. It's usually a slower build. But that slow and steady cadence of regular gifts can provide a release from the constant anxiety and pressure of end-of-year giving and major gifts.

So, how do you begin?

Good news—by reading this book you already have!

We'll start with developing the why behind your "product" and what structure makes sense based on the mission and goals of your organization.

WHY + STRUCTURE

When it comes to creating a product, there are a few key questions you need to ask right at the beginning:

- ➤ What's the reason for your product to exist?
- ➤ What's the impact it's intended to have?
- ➤ What structure aligns with the mission and values of your organization?

Some organizations, like Dressember, were created for peak fundraising times.

Since 2013, Dressember has rallied together 280,000 people raising $18MM, all starting through a seasonal style challenge campaign. Every December, advocates from all around the world wear a different dress or tie every day and start a peer-to-peer campaign fundraising to raise awareness and funds to support victims and survivors of human trafficking. The primary focus of fundraising for that campaign is October through January.

When discussing the origin story of their monthly giving program and the reason it needed to exist, Marissa Marx, Senior Director of Partnerships & Programs, mentioned, "The one thing we were missing was a way to engage year-round. That's why we started The Collective. We have this amazing community of people that are passionate about human trafficking. Before The Collective, we were saying, OK, come alongside us from October to January, and then we'll see you next October. This was really a way of keeping them engaged year-round."

Dressember innovated their fundraising model to include recurring giving to not rely on a few key months of the year for donations.

Does your fundraising rely heavily on seasonal peer-to-peer giving like Dressember where a recurring model could help reduce the pressure of one campaign?

Circle:

YES   or   NO

> **MINDSET SHIFT:** I'm a big fan of a "recurring-first" fundraising approach—asking donors to give monthly from the initial ask.

CASE STUDIES

Daily Giving

15,000 Monthly Donors | 80% Retention Rate

Mission: To enable every Jew to easily give charity every single day.

An innovative example of how a recurring donor program can be structured is Daily Giving's model. Daily Giving is a Jewish organization that combines the gift of thousands of

"Daily Givers" into one massive donation every single day to the multiple organizations they support.

I was blown away to learn that Daily Giving operates on a fully recurring giving model. The whole idea at the inception of the organization was to create a $1/day membership with the purpose of providing their customers the experience of not going one day without giving back and doing good.

COO Arieh Friedner talked at length about how the compound impact of what they're doing makes people excited about it. "Our donors are not our donors. They're our customers. We serve them. The mission of Daily Giving and the purpose of its existence is to help people automate their charity as if to say, 'How could I possibly go one day without giving to charity?' I'd rather give $1/day so that every day can be uplifted. And if we can use technology to automate that for them, then it's an important service that people need to be able to utilize. That's how the donors are our customers: we serve them by doing that."

Daily Giving's idea of a recurring-only approach didn't just work—it caught fire.

Daily Giving has an estimated 15,000 monthly supporters that help support seventy-eight nonprofits—and growing! I love, love, love how Arieh talks about their impact: "Our primary benefit is giving people the privilege of giving to charity every day, and the impact of the $14 million that goes to various needs within the Jewish community is because of that."

ANSWER THE FOLLOWING QUESTIONS FOR YOUR ORGANIZATION:

1. Does a recurring-first approach fit what your needs are?
2. Would this model excite your supporters?
3. Does it align with who they are?

This concept might seem scary at first, but as you've seen from Daily Giving, they've communicated it in a way where people are in!

The next two examples that have a powerful why and structure behind their recurring programs are organizations I personally support.

On International Women's Day, I knew I wanted to become a new monthly supporter for two women-led organizations. I wanted one to be local to the Atlanta area, where I live, and the other could be anywhere.

I honestly didn't have a set cause or mission in mind. I waited to see what popped up that day and compelled me to give.

While scrolling on LinkedIn, I came across a post from Gloria Umanah, the founder of the Hope Booth. Their mission is to provide individuals with an innovative, interactive, and immersive experience to encounter hope, affirm their dignity, and serve as a connection point to finding help and support on their journey to mental health.

The Hope Booth is a remodeled telephone booth that provides a three-minute interactive immersive experience that delivers artistic messages of hope strategically placed throughout the world to make hope accessible and affordable 24/7. The experience was developed and created with a science board of licensed professional psychologists, therapists, and social workers. The very first Hope Booth is just about forty minutes from my house at Ponce City Market.

From her post, I went to their website and was immediately pulled in with a bold statement on the home page: "For the next 3 minutes, be here." Right below that statement played a video that felt like it was meant just for me. It was an example of what you would watch when experiencing a Hope Booth.

The video called me in. I was hooked.

There was a button hovering on the home page with the words, "Join the Movement." It opened a Givebutter donation form, and I did just that. I joined the movement. I reached out to Gloria and had to let her know how impressed I was with everything she had created.

She expressed, "If I could go back in time, I would have paid more attention to our monthly supporters earlier on. Their consistent support has proven to be incredibly valuable. I wish we had recognized sooner how essential it is to nurture and grow those relationships because these donors are the heart and soul of our sustainability."

"If I could go back in time, I would have paid more attention to our monthly supporters earlier on."

Now, the Hope Booth is leading with recurring giving!

"Monthly giving is the foundation of our sustainability. Our recurring donors are a crucial part of ensuring that we can continue to serve our community consistently, regardless of the unpredictability of grants or one-time donations. They truly form the backbone of our mission, providing us with the security to dream bigger and make a deeper impact."

Every month I've been a supporter of The Movement, I've received a handwritten thank-you card! It's an incredibly thoughtful touch that they've considered in the structure of their program.

Like the Hope Booth, let this be a wake up call to what's possible when you activate a subscription for good.

Quick pause...let's walk through my donor's journey here.

1. I was connected to Gloria on LinkedIn and saw a post she wrote on LinkedIn on International Women's Day—great thought leadership approach to remain top-of-mind
2. I visited a beautifully designed website
3. There was a short and compelling video show-casing the experience of the Hope Booth
4. It was simple and clear on how to give monthly to The Movement
5. They illustrated WHY monthly giving was so important to them
6. I had never made any gift to this organization before this moment

We'll dive into each aspect of this journey in the following chapters, but take a moment to think through for your organization, how would a potential donor feel at each step I listed above?

The second organization I decided to give to on International Women's Day was the Chamber of Mothers. Their monthly giving program is called The Matriarchy. As a new mama, their mission spoke directly to my soul: uniting mothers as advocates to create a better America. With a focus on paid family leave, affordable childcare, and maternal health, this was in perfect alignment with my values. With an Instagram account of 65,000 and growing, this community has a groundswell of attention from women all over the country.

This virality created the perfect opportunity for a monthly giving program. When speaking with nonprofit strategist Jessica Campbell, she shared, "It didn't matter if the donation was $5 or $50—it was all about creating a movement. Our monthly donors, even those giving just $5, wanted to be a part of something bigger. They believe in our mission, and that belief translates into loyalty and consistent support. We've witnessed firsthand how even the smallest contributions, when pooled together, can make a significant impact.

We emphasize that every donation matters, and it's this mindset that's helped us build a movement of supporters who understand that their monthly gifts, regardless of size, contribute directly to the change we're making in the world."

Having a dedicated community of recurring supporters correlated directly to how their mission needed to operate.

Campbell explained, "We needed flexible funding that allowed us to pivot and allocate resources where they were most needed. Our monthly giving program provided that flexibility, giving us a steady stream of income we could rely on without the restrictions that often come with grants or project-based funding.

By establishing a strong base of monthly donors, we could confidently invest in new programs, respond quickly to emerging needs, and maintain the crucial infrastructure required to keep our organization running smoothly. This type of funding ensured that we were always prepared to tackle challenges head-on and seize opportunities as they arose."

Every organization has its own reason for the WHY and structure behind its program. What's yours?

→ **To Fill the Gap Between Annual Campaigns**—Imagine your organization as a ship navigating the high seas of non-profit work. During annual campaigns, it's like catching a big wave that propels you forward with a surge of funding. But what happens when that wave subsides? The waters can get pretty calm, even a bit stagnant. That's where a monthly giving program comes in. It's like having a steady breeze that keeps your sails filled, ensuring you can keep moving smoothly even between those big waves. With regular, predictable income, you can cover everyday expenses, tackle unexpected challenges, and keep your projects afloat all year round.

→ **To Build a Movement of Individuals**—Picture your cause as a vibrant, growing community. Every new monthly donor is like adding a new neighbor to the block. Over time, these neighbors become friends who truly care about each other and the community's well-being. By encouraging people to give regularly, you're not just collecting donations; you're building a loyal crew of supporters who are deeply invested in your mission. They're more likely to volunteer, spread the word, and stay with you for the long haul. This sense of belonging transforms your supporters into passionate advocates, each one contributing to a larger movement united by a common goal.

→ **To Only Accept Recurring Gifts**—Sometimes, simplicity is key. By focusing solely on recurring gifts, you're setting the stage for a clear, straightforward fundraising strategy. It's like running a subscription service where everyone knows what to expect and feels a consistent connection to your cause. This approach can make your fundraising efforts more predictable and stable, allowing you to plan bigger and bolder projects with confidence. Plus, it cuts down on the need for constant fundraising appeals, freeing up your time and energy to focus on making a real impact.

→ **Because Your Mission Needs Funds for Maintenance or More Flexible Funding**—One-time donations are great, but they often don't cover the ongoing costs of keeping everything in top shape. A monthly giving program is like having a dedicated team of mechanics who ensure everything runs without a hitch. Whether you're maintaining a shelter, operating a clinic, or supporting continuous research, steady funding is essential. Plus, monthly donations give you the flexibility to respond to needs as they arise, allocate funds where they're most needed, and invest in new opportunities to advance your mission.

All of the above or something entirely different?

FILL IN THE BLANK:

Our why is:

_____

_____

_____

Ideas for the structure of our program:

_____

_____

_____

Once you feel good about the why and structure of your product, it's time for one of my favorite parts of the framework...creating the identity.

NAMING PROCESS

This is often a place where organizations get stuck.

What in the world do we name this product, this program?

There's also another school of thought that monthly giving programs shouldn't be named anything at all.

I believe having a name is important.

> *A name creates recognition, trust, and community. And sometimes the best ideas come right from your community.*

The other day, while I was driving my car to pick up my daughter from daycare, I noticed a mother and her son in the car next to me rearranging a row of ducks that had taken over their entire dashboard. I found out that there is a proud community of Jeep owners who participate in a unique tradition called "ducking" or "duck duck Jeep." This tradition involves placing a rubber duck on another person's Jeep as a sign of respect to the owner of the vehicle. When you buy a Jeep, you're joining an entire microcommunity of fellow Jeep owners.

Who created this tradition?

It wasn't Jeep! It started in 2020 in Ontario, Canada. The trend began when a Jeep owner named Allison Parliament decided to spread some positivity during the early days of the COVID-19 pandemic. After experiencing a stressful encounter, she placed a rubber duck on another Jeep with a note, which quickly caught on and became a fun way for Jeep owners to connect and spread goodwill.

At the recent Classy Collaborative conference where hundreds of nonprofits gathered in Chicago, Classy President and GoFundMe COO Soraya Alexander spoke about the need for nonprofits to act as Chief Community Officers.

Release a bit of control and let your community create "moments" that will, in turn, grow your movement.

Release a bit of control and let your community create

"*moments*"

that will, in turn, grow your movement.

Jeep could have reached out and tried to shut the whole thing down, but they didn't. Instead, Jeep embraced this trend and even incorporated it into their marketing. For instance, during the North American International Auto Show, Jeep featured a giant rubber duck, symbolizing their support for the community-driven initiative. The company also used the #duckduckjeep hashtag to promote new models like the Wrangler Rubicon, further integrating the ducking trend into their brand culture.

I'm not part of this cool duck Jeep gang with my RAV4, but this is the point. If a car was just a car with no name, there would be no community built or branding. And surely no super cute rubber ducks chillin' on the dashboard of Jeeps around the world.

MINDSET SHIFT: Giving your program a name gives you the ability to build a brand around your product, create engaging marketing materials, talk about it in a completely different way, lend credibility, and develop recognition.

Let's put this to the test.

How do you feel after reading these two different asks?

"Will you give to charity: water's monthly giving program to end the water crisis?"

"Will you be part of The Spring to end the water crisis?"

One sounds very transactional, and the other makes me feel like I'm part of something bigger than myself. As humans, we crave connection and belonging. A name helps to provide those elements to a product.

Great. You know you need a name...but you're stuck on how to get the brainstorming process started.

I got you!

I developed an exercise that I walk all of my Monthly Giving Mastermind clients through that I did an iteration of years ago when creating the name for my company, Positive Equation.

I'll never forget sitting on the subway in NYC with the notes app open on my iPhone just writing whatever words came to me when brainstorming the name for my business. I started listing all the words I wanted my brand to encompass.

I knew I wanted to work with nonprofits and social impact companies on content that would make people feel good and create a positive impact.

Enter: Positive

Then I kept thinking about all the different parts of marketing—you need this + this + that to end up with a formula that works. The perfect equation.

Enter: Equation

In 2017, I named my business Positive Equation.

With the mastermind group, they get to go through an elevated version of this process together.

NAMING EXERCISE

Picture this: a group of passionate nonprofit professionals, all eager to create an engaging and memorable name for their monthly giving programs. We gather for a ninety-minute virtual call where the brainstorming magic begins. Everyone shares the intent behind their programs, and I open up a virtual Post-it note board in Canva. Then, with a series of prompts, we dive into a creative frenzy. I set a timer, and everyone starts jotting down words and phrases that resonate with their organization's mission and values, filling their respective Post-it notes with potential names and ideas. It's a fun, collaborative process that not only sparks creativity but also fosters a sense of community among the participants.

On the virtual board in Canva, I list the following questions to provide context for the brainstorm:

1. How would you describe your monthly giving program?
2. What makes it different?
3. What impact does it create?
4. How does someone feel when they join?
5. What's your organization's personality?
6. Are there any numbers, dates, or names of significance?
7. Is your first impression of the name strong?
8. Is it easy to read and pronounce?
9. Say "I joined _____" or "I'm a part of _____" or "I belong to _____." How does it sound?
10. Does it relay and speak to who you are?
11. Can it be recognizable?

Your turn! Set a timer for five to ten minutes and see what you come up with!

If you find yourself stuck, I have a free Monthly Giving Naming Exercise you can download at positiveequation.com/book.

After the initial brain dump of words, we set another timer and spend another five minutes or so providing suggestions to the other members of the group. This is one of my favorite parts of a mastermind—when you're collectively helping to influence and provide different perspectives to someone's work.

Once we have a ton of ideas for each organization, I have a bunch of emojis (hearts, smiley faces, stars, thumbs up) on the board that, as a group, we start to go through each virtual Post-it note and place emojis on the notes with words we feel resonate for their mission. There's usually a grouping of emojis around two to three words that are community favorites. Those get bulked together for a discussion. From those final words, a couple name options are created.

We go back to the questions above and review if it feels aligned with the "why" and purpose of the program. The organization takes those names back to their internal teams for further discussion and a vote!

At the time of writing this book, my mastermind group has helped name and create fifteen monthly donor programs:

1. The Roots
2. The Bench
3. The Essentials
4. Joyraisers
5. The Promise
6. The Party
7. The Table
8. The Pink Society
9. The Path
10. The Beacon
11. The Beat
12. The Trellis

13. The Village
14. Builders Guild
15. RISE

Each of these names helps tell a greater story about their mission.

It's not always a straightforward process, and names can evolve as your organization does. Let's take a look at a couple of organizations that ended up changing the name of their monthly giving programs to better reflect their mission and align with supporters.

CASE STUDIES

Roots Ethiopia: The Roots

187 Monthly Donors | 72% Retention Rate

Mission: Supports community identified solutions for job creation and education in Ethiopia.

When Roots Ethiopia joined the Monthly Giving Mastermind in 2022, they had an existing name for their program, "Grow," that sat idle and never really took off. The name, while meaningful, just didn't resonate or capture the imagination of potential supporters. During our naming exercise, Meghan Walsh, the Executive Director, took multiple ideas back to her board of directors. The board was enthusiastic about selecting an Ethiopian word to identify the name of the group, believing it would reflect the organization's cultural roots and mission authentically.

Meghan shared their initial choice: "It was Meseret—Amharic for foundation, the roots; the vessel." The word "Meseret" held significant meaning and seemed like a fitting choice. However, after much discussion and reflection, Meghan sought further counsel from the mastermind community. This group, composed of individuals outside the immediate circle of the organization, provided invaluable insights. They represented a broader audience perspective, akin to the potential donors Roots Ethiopia aimed to attract.

Through this collaborative process, it became evident that while "Meseret" was deeply meaningful, it might present challenges in pronunciation and recognition for a global audience. The mastermind community's feedback highlighted the importance of simplicity and clarity in a program name. Ultimately, Roots Ethiopia decided to go with "The Roots." This name maintained the essence of the original idea while ensuring it was easy to pronounce and understand without explanation.

Meghan reflected on this process: "With a lot of counseling from you and also the community who were part of the mastermind and leaning into what they really responded to, which they are a better representation of who would be looking at joining the program, we ended up going with The Roots."

The lesson here is clear: getting an outsider's perspective is crucial because we're often too close to our missions to see them objectively. When it comes to naming a program, you want it to be easy to pronounce and spell with no explanation needed. Engaging with a diverse group of advisors can provide the clarity and direction needed to select a name that not only aligns with your mission but also appeals broadly and effectively to your target audience.

Who can you ask to review your selected names?

_____

_____

_____

_____

_____

Chamber of Mothers: The Matriarchy

172 Monthly Donors | 100% Retention Rate[3]

Mission: To unite mothers as advocates to create a better America.

When I joined The Matriarchy, the Chamber of Mothers' monthly giving program, I was immediately struck by the boldness of the name. It felt strong and unapologetic, perfectly encapsulating the spirit of the organization. Curious about the origin story, I spoke with their nonprofit strategist, Jessica Campbell, who shared their creative process.

Jessica explained, "We created a Google Doc called No Bad Ideas. We have this amazing group of co-founders, really smart, thoughtful women. I sent it to them with a short description to brainstorm and set a deadline. This step is crucial because organizations can get stuck on a name indefinitely."

3   Launch was in May 2023 with no churn rate as of the publication of this book.

The collaborative effort resulted in a list of around forty-five names. To narrow it down, they used a fun and engaging method: voting with emojis. "We landed on the one that had the most votes. Originally, we had selected 'The Mother Council.' Then we tested it, and it wasn't rolling off the tongue. We wanted it to be strong, powerful, and on-brand," Jessica continued.

The discussion around the final name was intense. Some felt that the word "matriarchy" could be perceived as too extreme. However, the team ultimately embraced this boldness. "There was discussion that the use of the word 'matriarchy' could be seen as too extreme, but that's what we want. We want to repel the people that will be offended by that word, and we want to strongly attract people that are like, 'hell yeah!'"

The name The Matriarchy resonates deeply with their target donor demographic, embodying strength and unapologetic empowerment. By choosing a name that is both powerful and provocative, they set the tone for their mission and values, making it clear who they are and what they stand for.

The name itself acts as a filter, attracting individuals who are passionate about female empowerment and social justice and who are not afraid to stand behind a cause that challenges the status quo. It conveys a sense of solidarity and community among supporters, fostering a feeling of belonging to something greater than themselves. It sends a message that this is not just another charitable program but a movement with a bold vision.

The impact of a name that resonates on such a deep level cannot be understated; it helps build a strong, dedicated community of donors who are committed to sustaining the organization's mission over the long-term.

TIPS FOR THE NAMING PROCESS:

- **Involve Your Team:** Collaborate with your team and stakeholders. Their diverse perspectives can provide valuable insights and ideas.
- **Test Your Names:** Once you have a shortlist, test the names with a small group of supporters or volunteers. Get feedback on their initial impressions and feelings about the names.
- **Think Long-Term:** Consider how the name will evolve with your organization. Will it still be relevant and resonant in five or ten years?
- **Check for Availability:** Ensure that the name isn't already in use by another organization. Check domain availability if you plan to create a dedicated website or page for your program.
- **Stay True to Your Brand:** Make sure the name aligns with your overall branding and messaging. It should feel like a natural extension of your organization.

COMMON PITFALLS TO AVOID:

- **Overcomplicating the Name:** A name that's too complex or hard to pronounce can be a barrier. Aim for simplicity and clarity.

➜ **Ignoring Stakeholder Input:** While it's important to have a strong vision, ignoring valuable feedback from your team and supporters can lead to missed opportunities for a more resonant name.

➜ **Rushing the Process:** As much as I don't want you to get stuck here, naming is a critical step that requires thoughtful consideration. Avoid rushing through it just to move on to the next task.

➜ **Being Too Generic:** A generic name can make it hard to stand out. Strive for something unique that captures the essence of your program.

Naming your monthly giving program is a blend of creativity and strategy. It's your chance to craft a brand that not only resonates with your supporters but also embodies the essence of your mission. Take your time, involve your team, and have fun with the process.

Remember, the name is just the starting point—what you do with it will make your program truly impactful.

By following these steps and considering the examples provided, you'll be well on your way to naming a monthly giving program that not only stands out but also fosters a strong sense of community and purpose among your supporters.

In the next chapter, we'll dive into making the process seamless for supporters to take the action of becoming recurring donors.

AHA Moments!

1. **Treat Your Program as a Product:** Approach your monthly giving program like any other product launch. This means developing a solid marketing strategy, dedicating a budget, and having a passionate team to promote it. By thinking of it as a product, you'll be better equipped to attract and retain loyal donors.

2. **Knowing The Purpose:** Understanding the why behind your program and its structure is crucial for creating a successful monthly giving initiative. Knowing the purpose and impact of your program ensures it aligns with your mission and resonates with supporters. A well-defined structure helps sustain engagement and provides the flexibility needed to address ongoing needs, making your program more effective and resilient in achieving its goals.

3. **Naming and Branding Matter:** The name of your monthly giving program should reflect your mission, evoke a sense of belonging, and be easy to pronounce and spell. A memorable name helps build a brand around your program, creating engaging marketing materials and fostering a community of dedicated supporters.

NEXT STEPS:

_____

_____

_____

_____

_____

_____

_____

_____

_____

_____

_____

_____

_____

_____

_____

_____

_____

_____

_____

_____

_____

_____

_____

_____

CHAPTER 7
Step 2: Make It Easy

WHEN DINNERTIME ROLLS around in our house, usually the last thing I want to do is cook, so the meal delivery service HelloFresh has been a great answer for us to have healthy, delicious meals without having to plan it all out. Signing up for the service is a piece of cake! There's lots of customizable options, you can pick out the exact meals you want, the day of the week you want it delivered, and I can do it all while I'm running errands on the go.

How easy, yet personalized, can you make your giving experience for donors?

This chapter will delve into the importance of simplifying the recurring donation process for your supporters all the way from the first transaction to gift management. We'll explore how creating a professional, user-friendly interface can build trust and credibility, ensuring potential donors feel confident and excited to support your cause.

In a world where online shopping and one-click purchases have become the norm, your donation process—and management process—should all feel easy. Today's donors expect a seamless and intuitive experience that mirrors their everyday consumer interactions.

From optimizing your website's design to selecting the right donation tools, you'll learn practical strategies to eliminate friction and boost conversion rates. By the end of this chapter, you'll have the knowledge to transform your donation process into a smooth, engaging journey that delights donors and keeps them coming back.

> *"Make It Easy" is the crucial moment where the act of saying, "I'm in," takes place.*

This is the point where a potential donor has decided to take action and support your cause. If the donation process is complicated and confusing, it can lead to frustration and even abandonment of the donation. This is why it's important to have a seamless and user-friendly donation process, similar to the one-click-to-buy button on Amazon, to ensure that potential donors follow through with their decision to support your cause.

THE ROI OF GOOD BRANDING

I've had multiple conversations with friends who are graphic designers who share the struggle of proving the ROI of good branding.

But the truth is, it's invaluable.

MINDSET SHIFT: A well-designed website and social media presence can be seen as the storefronts for many nonprofits. In a world where physical visits to a nonprofit's location are not always possible, the majority of supporters will interact with the organization digitally.

As mentioned in the previous chapter, one of my Monthly Giving Mastermind alumni is the Board Chair of Roots Ethiopia, Meghan Walsh. When we first started working together, they had an existing monthly giving program called Grow. There was a landing page, but it was pretty bare-bones, outlining different giving levels with a donate button.

"The Roots has its own landing page with a clear message and platform, making it easier for donors to understand the impact they can make through their monthly support. It's a special, dedicated community of donors, and we have a steady practice of inviting people to join. Our website is now the space where we host people to come and donate, providing every opportunity to become a monthly donor or learn about The Roots."

MONTHLY GIVING LANDING PAGE = AVOIDING DONOR CONFUSION

A specific website for your monthly giving program not only creates a positive first impression but also establishes clarity, credibility, and trust in the eyes of potential donors.

I want to emphasize clarity.

Many nonprofits fear that emphasizing monthly giving might confuse or even deter donors. They worry about complaints or backlash from donors who might feel "tricked" into making a recurring donation. I've heard from numerous organizations that they receive messages from angry donors saying they didn't mean to make a monthly gift and felt deceived. This fear is understandable, but it's also addressable.

When you have a dedicated website that exclusively talks about your monthly giving program, mentions it by name, and offers only the option to give regularly, it significantly reduces confusion. Clear, focused communication on such a platform ensures that donors are fully aware of what they're committing to.

MINDSET SHIFT: Here's the truth— sometimes people make mistakes or decide they don't want to do monthly giving after all. That's okay! By having a clear, dedicated site for your monthly giving program, you've done your due diligence in providing all the necessary information upfront. This transparency not only builds trust but also empowers donors to make informed decisions, reducing the likelihood of negative feedback.

If you do get a message asking for cancellation, here's a sample email response. (Please edit in your own voice.)

Hi [Donor's Name],

I hope this email finds you well! First and foremost, I want to extend a heartfelt thank you for your recent donation to [Organization Name]. Your support means the world to us, and we truly appreciate your generosity.

I noticed that you might have intended to make a one-time donation but accidentally set it up as a monthly recurring gift. Mistakes happen, and I'm here to help you with whatever you'd like to do next.

Here are a couple of options:

***Keep Your Monthly Gift:** If you'd like to continue with the monthly donation, we'd be incredibly grateful. Your ongoing support would have a significant impact, helping us [briefly describe what the monthly donation would support, e.g., "provide meals for children," "sustain our community outreach programs," etc.]. We'd love to have you as part of our monthly giving community, (name)!*

***Cancel the Recurring Donation:** If a one-time donation was your intention, no worries at all! I'm here to assist you in canceling the monthly donation. Just let me know, and I'll take care of it right away.*

If you decide to keep the monthly donation, please know that you'll be making a lasting difference, and you'll receive regular updates on how your support is helping us achieve our mission. If not, we completely understand and appreciate your support in any form.

Please reply to this email and let me know how you'd like to proceed. I'm here to make this as easy as possible for you.

Thank you once again for your kindness and generosity.

WEBSITE FORMAT, EXPERIENCE, & ACCESSIBILITY

On my podcast, *Missions to Movements*, I interviewed Paige Chenault Lohoefer, Founder of The Birthday Party Project, about the rebrand of their logo and website they invested in at the beginning of COVID. She remarked, "It was one of the greatest investments we've made. It brought new energy and made it feel like the national brand we were. Partners started to pay attention too. When we elevated our brand, their confidence grew with us."

Having a well-designed web page for your recurring giving "product" is paramount. What storefront do you want to present to potential supporters?

If you walked into Nike and shoes were all over the floor and shirts were drooping over one another, would you want to spend time there shopping?

If the register was hidden down the aisle without signage, would you give up trying to check out?

> **Remember this is your digital storefront, often the ONLY experience and first impression someone will have of your organization.**

Will someone enjoy the experience on your site enough to linger around, clicking from page to page to learn more?

The web presence is *so so* important, and that's why I start every Monthly Giving Mastermind engagement with an audit and assessment of their current website.

AUDIT YOUR WEBSITE & DONATION EXPERIENCE

When performing these audits for my clients, one of my initial steps is to check their website's performance using a free tool called Microsoft Clarity. This tool can be easily embedded into your website, and it offers invaluable insights into user behavior. By utilizing Microsoft Clarity, you can view a heat map of where users tend to drop off the page while scrolling and track their mouse movements as they navigate the site. Once we've identified where users are dropping off, it's important to make sure we move any necessary elements above "the fold."

In web design, the fold refers to the part of a web page that is visible without scrolling. Everything above the fold is what a visitor first sees when they land on the page. This area is prime real estate for capturing attention and delivering your most important messages.

Surprisingly, in the majority of cases, a staggering 80% of users do not scroll past the fold. This means that if your key information, calls to action, or engaging content are buried below the fold, there's a high chance that most visitors will never see them.

Understanding where the fold lies on different devices (as it can vary between desktops, tablets, and mobile phones) is crucial. Microsoft Clarity helps you identify how far down the page users typically scroll, allowing you to adjust your content placement for maximum visibility and engagement.

By prioritizing essential elements above the fold—such as a compelling headline, your unique value proposition, and a clear call to action—you can increase the likelihood that visitors will engage with your content and take the desired actions. This approach not only enhances user experience but also boosts the overall effectiveness of your website in achieving its goals.

So, when it comes to designing your website, keep the fold in mind. Make sure the most critical elements are immediately visible to capture and retain the attention of your audience. This simple yet powerful strategy can significantly improve your website's performance and the success of your digital marketing efforts.

Let's do a self-audit together of your home page and monthly giving landing page—what should be there as we scroll down the page.

HOME PAGE

The Navigation Bar: Whether it has its own button or is under a dropdown, there should be access to your monthly giving program landing page across the site.

Home page Donation Form: There should be the option to toggle between one-time and monthly. Many donation tools now also have the automatic prompt to ask one-time supporters to switch their gift to monthly. This has proven to be a major growth tactic for a lot of organizations.

Featured Content: Is there a blog you can highlight or piece of content that references on the home page the importance of monthly giving to your organization? One of the websites I frequently reference is StJude.org. Right at the top of their home page is text that reads, "5 reasons to become a monthly donor," and it links out to a short blog with images of the kids and the ability to give.

MONTHLY GIVING LANDING PAGE OUTLINE

Having a dedicated landing page to express the importance and tell the impact story of your monthly donor community is paramount in making it easy.

MINDSET SHIFT: During a NextAfter webinar presented by John Powell, he said, "People react to web pages the same way we react to people." He went on to explain the parallels. The web page design relates to acceptance, the headline is the salutation, the sequence and length is the flow of conversation, etc. I love this because in the same way that someone can convince you to take action, a web page is essentially doing the exact same thing. He continued to explain, "The web page has to facilitate a great mental conversation."

How does this transfer to the necessary parts of a web page dedicated to your monthly donor program?

Thanks to the brilliance of HeartSpark Design's founder Lauren Atherton, my team has built fifteen monthly donor landing pages based on two different templates clients can choose from.

Both templates include the following core elements:

Main Headline: What are your donors helping to make possible? What's your BIG bold vision statement? We'll go more in depth on how to craft your headline in Step 3: Call in the Believers, but here you want to articulate the problem and how you uniquely solve it. What makes YOUR organization different? This one line should simply answer the question, "What do you do?"

Subheader: Briefly detail the issue and what their monthly gift will do to change that.

Image: Visually showcasing what you're describing, leading with hope.

Donation Tool (in the header): Form or button elements that pop up (not going to a separate page!)

Benefits: Will you send monthly emails? A special video series? A quarterly impact report? Is there a special item someone receives when joining? MANNA, a nonprofit that provides medically tailored meals and nutrition education to people with serious illnesses in Philadelphia, gifts a branded apron to monthly supporters that join the "MANNA F.A.M."

When you join Every Shelter's monthly giving program, The Haven, at $30/month, you receive a tote bag. But this tote bag is special. Every Shelter designs shelter for refugees, so on The Haven landing page, they explain one of their shelter solutions is from discarded billboard vinyl. With the billboard scraps, a refugee partner makes the tote bags!

How brilliant and cool is that?!

I'm not saying you need to have a gift or something you send when someone joins your program, but it creates another opportunity to share your mission. We'll talk about this more in Step 5: Share Constant Joy & Gratitude.

Video: A video is optional, but a powerful one gives someone the opportunity to get to know you within a matter of minutes. According to a blog post from DonorBox, viewers retain 95% of a message when conveyed through video, compared to just 10% through text. And a substantial 57% of people who watch nonprofit videos proceed to make a donation. This statistic underscores the persuasive power of visual storytelling in converting viewers into donors.

In the nonprofit world, one of the most famous videos that continues to draw in thousands of monthly donors is The Spring by charity: water.

Content Lead, Cubby Graham spoke to the dramatic impact the video had on the program: "We launched The Spring as a global community, like a family for anyone anywhere to join to fight the water crisis. But it wasn't until we released our video that people really started to see the impact they could make.

The video showed the transformation of communities before and after getting access to clean water, and it moved people profoundly. It connected them emotionally to the cause and showed them the tangible change their donations could bring about. That video alone helped us double our Spring membership numbers in just a few months."

Donate Button: Throughout the page, multiple donation options should be available. Another reason for naming your program comes into play here. On the button, you can be way more intentional and creative with the wording.

Instead of "Donate Now," "Donate," or "Give," you can play off the name of your program:

→ Join the Builders Guild
→ Let's Build
→ Take a Seat at The Table
→ RISE with Us
→ Join Us on The Path

See what I mean? Transactional versus intentional.

How do you feel reading those versus seeing a standard "Donate" button?

You're being called to join a community.

Social Proof: There are many different angles you can use to activate social proof on your landing page. The strongest persuasion comes from our peers.

FOMO: The concept of FOMO, or "fear of missing out," is a powerful motivator when it comes to persuading potential donors. By creating a sense of urgency, such as being one of the first fifty founding members or having a time-sensitive matching opportunity, you tap into people's innate desire to be a part of something exclusive and time sensitive. This can be a highly effective way to activate social proof on your landing page and encourage people to donate.

Examples:

→ Limited-Time Offers: "Only a few days left!" or "While supplies last!" For your organization, this could be

> We launched The Spring as a global community, like **a family for anyone anywhere to join to fight the water crisis.**

Cubby Graham
Content Lead
charity: water

a matching gift that's only available for a certain time period or a special founding member perk.

➜ Exclusive Access: Promoting early-bird access or members-only benefits.

➜ Social Media Highlights: Showcasing real-time events or experiences that others are participating in, creating a sense of missing out.

By utilizing FOMO, you are not only appealing to individuals' desire to be a part of a community, but you are also tapping into their fear of being left out. This fear can be a powerful driving force in motivating people to take action, especially when combined with the persuasive influence of social proof from their peers.

The Herd Mentality: "Birds of a feather flock together." We sure do! The herd mentality can be a powerful tool in motivating people to take action. As social creatures, we have a strong desire to be a part of a community and feel connected to others. This desire is often heightened during moments of crisis or when faced with a common cause. However, it is not just our need for community that drives us to take action but also our fear of being left out. The thought of being the only one not participating or contributing can be a powerful motivator, pushing us to join in and be a part of the herd.

Examples:

➜ **Best-Selling Products:** Promoting products as "bestsellers" to show that many others are buying them.

- **Crowded Events:** Highlighting the popularity of an event by showcasing large attendance numbers. The Adventure Project's monthly giving program, The Collective, utilizes an example of the herd mentality right within their header section: "Join 381 incredible people by signing up this month." Reading that, I feel SO compelled to be number 382!

- **Customer Reviews:** Displaying numerous positive reviews to show widespread approval. When's the last time you made a purchase based off reading reviews? Every time I go to book an AirBnB, it's one of the first things I check. This highlights how much supporters love being part of the program, and it's a special way for them to feel valued.

When we see others around us giving or taking action, it validates our own desire to do the same. We may question our own thoughts and beliefs, but when we see others doing the same thing, we feel more confident in our decision to follow suit. This is why we often see a domino effect when it comes to giving or taking action. One person's actions can inspire others to do the same, creating a powerful force for change.

When's the last time you were at a restaurant, heard your friend order a drink, thought it sounded good, and soon enough your whole table was having the same beverage? The same is true in giving.

During the holidays, our local Hobby Lobby has the Salvation Army bell ringers, and as I approach the doors watching others giving, there's no way I'm not reaching into my wallet to see what spare change or dollars I have! We've seen this play out with national disasters, acts of war, and large social movements like "Black Lives Matter" and "Me Too." It taps into our innate desire to be a part of a community and our fear of being left out. By understanding and harnessing this mentality, we can inspire and motivate others to join in and make a difference.

While both herd mentality and FOMO leverage social proof to influence behavior, they operate through different psychological triggers. Herd mentality relies on the safety and trust perceived in following the crowd, while FOMO capitalizes on the anxiety of missing out on something desirable. Understanding these differences will allow you to tailor strategies effectively to influence consumer behavior.

CUSTOM THANK-YOU PAGE

An often overlooked opportunity to gain more insights into who your supporters are is with a custom thank-you page. After the donation is made, check with your donation tool, but most allow you to redirect people to a custom thank-you page that's on your website. Knowing that this person just joined your monthly giving program, use this page to ask further questions!

Have a video with someone prominent within your community saying, "Thanks!" and have a simple form where you can ask a couple of quick questions like:

1. We're SO excited you're here. What made you decide to join "name of program"?
2. If you plan to send swag down the line, what's your t-shirt size?
3. If you didn't ask for their address in the donation form, you can make it more friendly here by saying, "We'd love to send you an official welcome. What's your address?"

Be creative here! It's right after they've made a big decision with you, continuing that joy and excitement.

OPTIMIZE YOUR DONATION TOOL

After you have the format of your website established, now you'll want to find a front-end donation solution that provides a stellar monthly giving experience.

You might be thinking, "Well, of course, our current donation tool has x, y, z...but does it create the right experience when it comes to recurring giving?" Let's troubleshoot. I've seen a lot of GREAT CRMs with so-so front-end giving tools, but that's why integrations and wonderful tools like Zapier exist to connect the dots.

Within the first two weeks of my Monthly Giving Mastermind, I go through a donation optimization audit of each organization's donation tool as a potential supporter.

THE FOLLOWING QUESTIONS ARE WHAT I ASK MYSELF WHEN GOING THROUGH THE AUDIT:

→ Was I able to find where to donate?

➔ Does it have a "monthly" only option (because I'm on the monthly program landing page)?

➔ Does it look intimidating, aka a long form?

➔ Am I sent to a different page to give or is the form embedded into the website?

➔ Is there the option of clicking a donate button that opens a pop-up to give?

➔ Do I have to enter all my contact information BEFORE saying "yes" to the gift?

➔ What payment options are available?

➔ Can I ask custom questions? Monthly donors are IN for the long haul, so this is a great opportunity to ask for birthday information, t-shirt size if you'll ever send swag, and why they decided to join the name of your program.

➔ What's the donor management experience like?

➔ Can I redirect to a custom thank-you page? This is also a great page to have a thank-you video from a key stakeholder of your organization with the ability to ask custom questions after the gift is made.

Following my analysis, I have one-on-one calls with each organization to discuss my findings. I always check if their current tool can be updated or optimized, and if not, suggest two to three other options that will seamlessly integrate with their CRM or other platforms.

Having the right tool is *so, so, so* important.

An example of this is with the Tim Tebow Foundation. For Tim Tebow's birthday, they ran their largest campaign that raised around $2 million from 13,000-14,000 donors. They noticed that 11% of those donors became recurring donors because their embedded donation tool had a pop-up that asked supporters to convert their gift in the moment to recurring instead of only 3-4% converting when asked separately.

> *If someone made their way from an ad, a social media post, a direct search on Google, or an email to your landing page, you want to make sure the final step of completing the gift is as EASY and seamless as possible.*

A great exercise to test if your donation experience is too clunky is to ask a friend who has never visited your website to go through the experience of making a monthly gift.

Most likely, they'll be testing this on mobile, but run the test on desktop as well.

- Can they find the landing page?
- How long did it take them to find it?
- Did they scroll once they got there?
- How many clicks have they made?
- Any confusion?
- How long is it taking them to make the donation?
- Did they know it was monthly?
- What payment methods were they offered?
- Were they prompted to cover any fees?
- What happens after the transaction?

Make notes, or better yet, record their screen to watch the actions back.

ABANDONED CART

Have you ever been in the middle of making a donation or purchase online, only to be interrupted by your kid waking up from a nap or maybe you got a phone call or you're just distracted? Happens to me all the time—and according to Shopify, I'm not alone. More than 70% of online shopping carts are abandoned before a customer makes a sale!

You intend to get back to it but sometimes forget. Then, out of the blue, you get an email reminding you to finish what you started. Ever wondered how they did that?

The magic of technology!

You entered your email address before getting distracted. That little piece of information allows the site to send you an abandoned cart email, nudging you to complete your transaction.

Many donation tools offer this feature, but one that stands out is Fundraise Up. They've integrated this functionality into their donation process. If you exit out of the donation pop-up, you'll see a prompt: "Please leave your email address below, and we'll send you a gentle reminder later." Plus, you can customize the follow-up email that goes out.

These subtle but impactful features can significantly boost your conversion rates.

When I first saw the data from the e-commerce world, I was amazed, though it made perfect sense when I thought about my own habits.

CONVERSION RATES

➔ **Open Rates:** Abandoned cart emails generally have high open rates, often between 40% and 50%.

➔ **Click-Through Rates:** The click-through rates for abandoned cart emails are also impressive, typically ranging from 10% to 20%.

➔ **Conversion Rates:** Approximately 10% to 15% of users who receive an abandoned cart email go on to complete their purchase.

RECOVERY RATES

➔ **Revenue Recovery:** On average, abandoned cart emails can recover 10% to 30% of lost revenue. This means for every $1000 in abandoned carts, businesses can recover $100 to $300 by sending these emails.

➔ **Multiple Emails:** Sending a series of abandoned cart emails rather than just one can increase recovery rates. A typical sequence might involve sending three emails over a few days, each with increasing urgency or incentives.

TIMING AND PERSONALIZATION

➜ **Timing:** The timing of abandoned cart emails is critical. The first email should ideally be sent within an hour of cart abandonment, followed by subsequent reminders over the next twenty-four to forty-eight hours.

➜ **Personalization:** Personalized emails, which include details like the customer's name and the specific items they left in their cart, are more effective than generic emails. They can increase the likelihood of recovery by 26%.

These statistics highlight the power of abandoned cart emails in converting hesitant or distracted visitors into committed donors or customers.

For nonprofits, implementing a similar approach can turn potential supporters into recurring donors, increasing both immediate and long-term revenue.

I highly recommend reaching out to the platform that facilitates your donation checkout experience and see if this is something they already have available or is on their radar. If not, see if it's something they're willing to add to their new features list for development.

The initial gift is only the beginning of the interaction your supporter will have with you over the years to come.

MANAGING THEIR GIFT

Let's say you're a dedicated supporter of a nonprofit and give regularly. Life happens—maybe an unexpected expense arises, or perhaps you've received a raise and want to increase your donation. If the process to adjust your giving is cumbersome or unclear, it can lead to frustration and even deter you from continuing your support.

Remember my wonderful HelloFresh experience? When you've enjoyed their meals but need to cancel your subscription, that's another story! You open the mobile app, expecting to find an easy way to manage your account, only to discover that you must switch to the desktop version to cancel your subscription.

The process is not intuitive, and navigating through multiple steps on a different device is frustrating and time-consuming. This negative experience can leave a bad taste in your mouth, making you less likely to return or recommend the service to others.

Now, imagine if the same level of frustration was applied to managing regular donations. Donors could feel disrespected and unappreciated, potentially leading to higher cancellation rates and fewer long-term supporters.

Just as with any subscription service, the ability to easily manage your recurring donations is crucial. Donors should have the same level of control and convenience they experience with other online services. This kind of flexibility not only improves donor satisfaction but also enhances trust and loyalty towards your organization.

Arieh Friedner at Daily Giving spoke about how important this aspect of the giving process is to his team. He said:

"So first and foremost, you have to have the technical capacity to allow them a user-friendly experience. For example, we wanted to make sure we had a clear login process on our website, because if you can't intuitively see how to pause or cancel your account, then there might be a lack of trust. Then, every Thursday, the whole team gets together for "Journey to Zero.""

Journey to Zero is a meeting on everyone's calendar to make sure that everyone that has emailed their collective inbox gets answered. With 15,000 recurring accounts, there are always emails in there. Every single person that reaches out to them gets a timely response. Having a communication strategy, aka customer service plan, is key.

Reach out to your donation platform partner and see if a "Donor Portal" or something similar exists where supporters can manage their gifts. Donation tools have new features released all the time, and you might be using outdated functionality.

Whether you have one or 50,000 recurring donors, establishing a donor relations communications strategy is important. That could be a weekly team check-in like Daily Giving or setting a ten-minute calendar reminder daily for you to check your main email account and social channels.

With the format of your website in place and an understanding of what to think through when it comes to selecting your donation tool, it's time to call in your believers—because they're out there, just waiting to join you on this journey! In the next chapter, we'll uncover how to draw in your superfans.

AHA Moments!

1. **Seamless Donation Process:** In the era of one-click purchases, your donation process should be equally seamless and intuitive. A complicated and confusing process can frustrate potential donors, leading to abandoned donations. Ensure your donation experience is as easy as the one-click-to-buy button on Amazon to retain and convert more supporters.

2. **Importance of Professional Design:** A well-designed website for your program and social media presence act as storefronts for your nonprofit. In today's digital age, where many supporters interact with organizations online, having a professional, user-friendly interface builds trust and credibility, encouraging donors to feel confident and excited to support your cause.

3. **Optimize Website Layout:** Utilizing tools like Microsoft Clarity to assess website performance can provide invaluable insights. Ensure that your recurring donation program is prominently featured and easily accessible from various sections of your website. Crucial information should be readily available above the fold to capture visitors' attention and prompt immediate action.

4. **Flexibility for Donors:** Providing donors with the ability to easily manage their recurring donations—whether they need to increase, decrease, pause, or cancel—enhances

satisfaction and trust. Just as with any subscription service, a user-friendly experience is crucial. Avoid the frustration seen in commercial examples like HelloFresh, where managing subscriptions can be cumbersome and discouraging. Instead, offer clear and intuitive options that respect and accommodate donors' needs.

NEXT STEPS:

_____

_____

_____

_____

_____

_____

_____

_____

_____

_____

_____

_____

_____

_____

_____

_____

_____

_____

_____

CHAPTER 8
Step 3: Call in the Believers

I MARCHED DOWN the fifty-yard line, and all I heard was the buzz from the collective cheering of a sold-out crowd of 45,622 University of Central Florida (UCF) Knights football fans. The roar was deafening, a wave of sound that made my heart pound in my chest. In 2007, I was a freshman at UCF. GO KNIGHTS! I joined the marching band in the color guard, and on September 15th, I dressed in my black and gold sparkling uniform for our first on-campus football game against the University of Texas.

As I stood on the field, the energy was electric. I could barely hear the drumline or band over the thunderous applause and cheers. I only had cues from looking to my left and right to keep in line. The stadium was alive with excitement, and I felt a rush of adrenaline unlike anything I'd ever experienced.

It was electrifying. I was hooked.

The game itself was a nail-biter. What was thought to be a sure win by Texas turned out to be a very competitive game with fans on edge the entire time. The song "Kernkraft 400" by the electronic band Zombie Nation played, and it's like we all just knew what to do. The stands erupted, and we all started jumping and chanting the "woah-oh" melody over and over, "U-C-F KNIGHTS." The sight of thousands of fans moving in unison, creating a literal bounce in the stadium, was surreal. This game earned the stadium the nickname "The Bounce House," often captured by television cameras during national broadcasts.

On that day, I became a die-hard UCF football fan and believer in Knight Nation. We have a sea of UCF apparel in our house, including many baby onesies. I've been on the New York City and Atlanta Alumni Board, and I traveled to Ireland in 2014 when we played Penn State at Croke Park Stadium in Dublin to cheer on my Knights. No doubt, if I was being tracked in UCF's CRM, I'd be considered a superfan!

The game marked the beginning of my involvement and dedication to the UCF community. I found a sense of belonging and camaraderie in the sea of black and gold, surrounded by fellow Knights who shared the same passion for our team. I discovered the true meaning of being a part of something bigger than myself, and it was exhilarating.

From that day on, I never missed a home game and attended as many away games as I could. I was present for some of the biggest victories and heartbreaking losses, but my support never wavered. I even ended up marrying another Knight!

This personal journey mirrors what we aim to achieve with our monthly giving programs: creating a community of dedicated believers. Just as I found my place in Knight Nation, we want our donors to feel that same sense of belonging and passion for our cause.

Whether you're a collegiate football fan or not, there's no doubt it generates massive fandom and profits. For example, during the 2022-2023 season, the combined revenue of the SEC and Big Ten conferences alone topped $2 billion. Individual programs within these conferences also generate significant income, with Ohio State reporting total revenues of approximately $251.6 million, Texas at $239.3 million, and Alabama at $214.4 million!! College football remains a critical financial pillar for many universities, contributing to the sustainability and growth of their athletic programs and other institutional initiatives.

The concept of a season ticket holder is similar to being a monthly supporter of a cause. Major football programs at large universities can each have tens of thousands of season ticket holders, contributing significantly to their athletic department revenues.

The incentives are premium seating, special event invitations, swag, etc. Season ticket holders provide some forecasting of revenue for universities. Even as I wrote this, I realized I wrote "our team" and "my Knights." I have such an associated personal identity that I used possessive language.

We want to find YOUR believers. Your superfans.

This chapter is all about just that—laying the groundwork to attract those superfans who are truly passionate about your cause before making that all-important ask for a donation. I'll share some tactical strategies and case studies from organizations living out their mission through their supporters.

WHY SUPERFANS MATTER

Do you remember the iconic REI #OptOutside Black Friday campaign from 2015? They shocked consumers and fellow retailers when instead of the constant bombardment of ads to purchase products, they closed all 142 locations, suspended online sales, and paid employees to go outside and enjoy nature.

The campaign turned out to be a smashing success. On a day when state parks typically stay closed, hundreds of them opened their gates. Following REI's bold move, 170 other businesses and organizations also closed their doors. And the cherry on top? REI saw its highest Black Friday sales ever that weekend!

So, why did this daring move pay off so well?

Marcus Collins, an award-winning marketer who's worked with big names like Google, Nike, Beyoncé, and the Brooklyn Nets, says it all comes down to culture. In his book, *For the Culture: The Power Behind What We Buy, What We Do, and Who We Want to Be,* Collins explores how leveraging the power of congregations, rivalries, language, and meaning can build a strong community around your brand.

REI understood their die-hard consumers are people who want to be outdoors. So when they went against the grain of the commercialized Black Friday, they loved it!

MINDSET SHIFT: Instead of just looking for an audience, find a congregation.

REI's campaign was designed to appeal to their superfans—their congregation.

We all need superfans, avid believers, and loyalists that will raise their voice on our behalf. These are the folks who eat, sleep, and breathe your brand. They aren't just regular supporters; they're your brand ambassadors and early adopters to what's next!

These superfans form a vibrant community around your brand. They create a sense of belonging and camaraderie that draws in others, fostering deeper engagement. Their enthusiasm and glowing reviews convince others that your organization is the real deal—and they have to be part of it.

The bond they share with you is deeply personal. This deep connection fosters long-term loyalty and advocacy; even in times of crisis or negative publicity, these superfans stand by you, defending your brand and helping to maintain its reputation.

They are essential.

We all have different passions, interests, life experiences, traumas, etc., that guide our charitable giving. Your monthly giving program provides a sense of belonging, identity, community, and connection.

As Collins states in his book, "We don't build community, we facilitate it."

The nonprofit Miry's List understood this philosophy when they created Welcomer's Circle. The organization is made up of neighbors and friends dedicated to welcoming new arrival refugee families into the United States with the things that they need to get started in their new lives. This includes living necessities (diapers, beds, cleaning supplies, toiletries), but also the things that allow you to thrive in a new country, including English tutoring, playdates, social gatherings, shopping trips, career development, and mentoring.

Cyndi Otteson, Co-Founder and former Chief Development Officer, understood that having a monthly giving program in place would cultivate the people who are passionate about what they do: "People want to help. We're just a vessel. Yes, we're a nonprofit, but we're just a conduit to match people to the right people, and the right causes, and the right things, because the time, money, energy, it's all so that we can be in alignment with our values."

So, what does this look like in action? How do you call in your believers?

EMPOWER SUPPORTERS

When I started Positive Equation, one of my first clients was Movember. I helped run their social media and digital marketing efforts from 2017-2019.

Movember is the leading global charity changing the face of men's health, focused on mental health and suicide prevention, prostate cancer, and testicular cancer. If you notice a surge of moustaches every November, you can thank Movember!

People want to help. We're just a vessel ... a conduit to match people to the right people, and the right causes, and the right things, because the time, money, energy, **it's all so that we can be in alignment with our values.**

Cyndi Otteson
Co-founder, former CDO
Miry's List

The movement began in 2003 when Travis Garone and Luke Slattery from Melbourne, Australia, decided to bring back the moustache trend while raising money for prostate cancer. The initiative quickly grew, formalizing into the Movember Foundation.

Since its inception, with the support of six million Mo Bros and Mo Sisters from around the world, Movember has funded more than 1,320 men's health projects globally. The foundation's impact spans twenty countries, supporting vital research, raising awareness, and improving health outcomes for men worldwide.

How was a movement like this created?

They created an iconic brand deeply rooted in who they wanted to serve. They also made their Mo Bros and Mo Sisters the heroes with clever and direct copy.

On their website, they state, "They are the rock stars—we are the roadies."

What I noticed while working there was they empowered their Mo Bros and Mo Sisters to be creative in their fundraising efforts. Sure, they provided brand guidelines and materials. They created different ways people could get involved:

➔ Grow A Mo
➔ Move for Mental Health
➔ Host a Mo-Ment
➔ Mo Your Own Way

But the specifics? They left that up to their superfans! On their website it states: "Mo Your Own Way is your hall pass to embrace the weird, wild and unexpected. So go all-out. And remember: donations favor the brave. "

And *millions* have been up for the challenge!

➜ **Walker Winjum Moustachioed March:** Walker Winjum, a Movember Student Ambassador for North Dakota State University, took his fundraising efforts to the next level by organizing a march with his fraternity. They marched from Grand Forks, North Dakota, all the way to Fargo— that's eighty miles!! Twenty-four hours later, they raised over $7,000. This unique and grueling challenge attracted significant attention and donations, highlighting the lengths people will go to support Movember.

➜ **Matt Desilva's Decade Dedication:** ten-year Mo Bro Matt Desilva is the team captain and workplace lead for Team CVS Health. He's not only personally raised $45,000 but has also instilled the importance of men's health with CVS to create a corporate grant. His engaging approach not only raised substantial funds but also inspired many to join the cause and take proactive steps towards their health.

➜ **Kirsty Newsome's Challenge:** Kirsty, a Mo Sister from the UK, undertook an intense physical challenge for Movember. Each day, she completed either seventy-five push-ups, sixty sit-ups, twenty-six pull-ups, or 5583 meters of cardio, with each number representing a mental health statistic. Over the last three days of Movember, she combined all the workouts into one epic daily challenge. This creative and grueling effort not only raised substantial funds but also highlighted the critical issues in men's mental health.

Movember's brand leans into and celebrates the creativity of their supporters, building a following that's dedicated year after year.

How can you inspire, and provide the freedom, and support for donors to take a more personal approach to your mission?

Brainstorm some ideas here:

_____

_____

_____

_____

_____

Every day, we're bombarded with messaging while shopping in the grocery store, driving down the highway, watching TV, or scrolling on our phones. When someone takes the action to visit the website for your program, the copy needs to speak to your believers.

IMPORTANCE OF YOUR COPY

Writing powerful persuasive copy is an art form.

When we're too close to our mission, there's a trend I've noticed for most nonprofits—and this applies to any of us who are business owners too. We complicate any language about what we do.

If you're like me, you might have big ideas and a deep understanding of the mission, but when it comes to putting it into words, *we struggle*. That's where a skilled copywriter comes in. They can take our jumbled thoughts and transform them into powerful, persuasive copy that speaks to our target audience.

When it comes to attracting believers and die-hard fans, the copy on our website is crucial. It needs to be written in a way that resonates with them and speaks directly to their hearts. A good copywriter knows how to tap into the emotions of our audience and compel them to take action. So, while we may not consider ourselves great writers, investing in a skilled copywriter can make all the difference in the success of our program.

If you don't have the budget for a copywriter, here's one of my favorite DIY practices to come up with your big, bold headline for your monthly giving page.

I utilize the StoryBrand one-liner framework. It doesn't have to be one sentence, but it should be a concise, clear statement that captures the essence of what your organization does. It includes three parts: the problem you solve, your solution, and the positive result. This formula helps make your message straightforward and memorable.

For nonprofits, crafting a compelling one-liner for your monthly giving landing page is crucial. It quickly communicates the value of recurring donations, resonates with potential donors, and makes your mission easy to understand.

So let's put this into practice.

1. **Problem**: Identify the issue your organization addresses.
2. **Solution**: Explain how your nonprofit solves this problem.
3. **Result**: Describe the positive outcome or transformation.

Here's a one-liner example I drafted based on the work of Feeding Westchester's monthly giving program, Nourishing Neighbors.

Nearly 200,000 neighbors are turning to Feeding Westchester for food assistance each month. With food and housing prices on the rise, many are still struggling to make ends meet. Nourishing Neighbors brings nutritious food wherever it's needed most. We envision a community where all people have access to the food they need today and the fundamental resources to build a better tomorrow.

> **Problem:** Nearly 200,000 neighbors are turning to Feeding Westchester for food assistance each month. With food and housing prices on the rise, many are still struggling to make ends meet.

> **Solution:** Nourishing Neighbors brings nutritious food wherever it's needed most. (If they wanted to expand on this, they could include any specific dollar impact messaging: "For $30 you can feed a hungry neighbor for an entire month!")

Result: We envision a community where all people have access to the food they need today and the fundamental resources to build a better tomorrow.

This approach makes your message concise and engaging, which is perfect for a monthly giving landing page, drawing in potential donors by clearly articulating the impact of their support.

What's your one-liner that can be utilized as a headline for your website?

_____

_____

_____

_____

_____

_____

ACCESSIBILITY

Creating an accessible website means ensuring that everyone, including people with disabilities, can easily use and navigate your site.

Here are some key things to keep in mind:

1. **Ensure everyone can see and understand your content.** This means adding text descriptions to images and videos so those who can't see them still know what's going on. Your site should work in various formats without losing

any important details. And don't forget about making things easy to see and hear by ensuring good contrast between text and backgrounds.

2. **Your site should be operable.** Everything should be accessible with just a keyboard, giving folks who can't use a mouse the ability to browse. Allow enough time for users to read and interact with content, and avoid flashing elements that could trigger seizures. Navigation should be a breeze, helping users find what they need without hassle.

3. **Keep your text simple and readable**. Ensure pages behave in predictable ways, and help users fix any mistakes they make in forms.

For technical guidance, the Web Content Accessibility Guidelines (WCAG) are your go-to resource. Following their guidelines can help you hit different levels of accessibility.

COPYWRITING

Good copy should also be clear and speak to your target reader.

When I studied advertising and public relations, we were told that when writing marketing copy, it should be around sixth to eighth grade reading levels.

I led a workshop at Neumann University for about seventy nonprofits to help them prepare for their first local Giving Day Challenge. Before the event, I asked for a list of the attendees and did a mini website analysis of their home page language. Not the whole home page, just the initial copy, right in the main header. The first thing you see.

I used this handy free tool called the HemingwayApp. com to copy and paste the copy, and it generates a readability grade level.

The first organization I did an audit for was Girls on the Run. Their headline said:

> *"Girls on the Run has fun, evidence-based programs that inspire participants to recognize their inner strength, increase their level of physical activity, imagine their possibilities, and confidently stand up for themselves and others."*

Put it into the Hemingway App—grade twelve. And also, what does the sentence really mean??

Based on looking through their website, I took a stab at rewriting it:

> *Girls on the Run provides confidence-building programs for 3rd-8th grade girls that end with a 5k fun run!*

Reading level? Grade eight.

I then asked the staff member in the room, does this accurately explain what your organization does? She laughed and said, "It sure does!"

There are two donor bases I would niche down and look to attract here:

1. Families with third-to-eighth-grade-children
2. Female runners who have an interest in philanthropy.

The initial copy mentioned nothing about the specific age ranges they serve or the 5k fun run that's a big part of their program. If I have a third-to-eighth grade daughter or granddaughter, I'm now seeing an immediate personal connection.

Another example is our work with Friends of the Columbia Gorge.

In 2023, they joined the Monthly Giving Mastermind to refresh an existing recurring giving program they had in place. We rebranded the name of the program to The Beacon, named after the iconic Beacon Rock along the Columbia Gorge Trail. It's a well-known landmark to anyone who frequents the area. Their mission is to protect, preserve, and steward the Columbia Gorge. Their supporters value this beautiful land and the experiences it provides to them while visiting.

We wanted to ensure the website copy called in these believers.

The site reads:

Calling All Watch Dogs—We are a passionate group of visionaries who know that wanting to preserve the natural environment of the Columbia Gorge is well and good.

But taking action to protect the Gorge so it stays wild and wondrous is necessary.

When you become a member of The Beacon, your monthly gift goes right to the heart of our mission:

ensuring the Gorge remains a vibrant, living place that's open to all.

There are a few key words and phrases that stand out on purpose:

➤ Watch Dogs—on the lookout, keeping guard of a property.
➤ The use of "we" and "you"
➤ Wild and wondrous
➤ Vibrant, living place

We're not only calling out the things that the ideal monthly supporter loves about The Gorge and wants to see protected but also including them in the solution to make it happen. Addressing the reader as "watch dogs" and "visionaries" are terms a monthly supporter may already identify with as a proud protector of the land.

Roots Ethiopia's website follows a similar outline:

Unshakeable in Our Vision of a Poverty-Free World.

We are a group of people who see the future as a poverty-free world and who take action to make it so.

Community priorities are our priorities. That's why we give villages the help and resources they need to use their own Ethiopian skills, wisdom, and knowledge to become self-sustainable.

What stands out here?

The copy uses language that includes the reader in the mission: "We are" a group of people, "our priorities," "we give villages."

Are your wheels spinning? Have you opened your phone and started scrolling through your website yet?

And don't stop there!

This is a great exercise to use in all your email marketing and social media content as well.

➡ Are you using language that calls in your believers?
➡ That shares the values and vision you both want to see happen?
➡ What words do people often say about your organization, and why do they give?
➡ What inspires them?

Write them here!

_____

_____

_____

_____

_____

_____

Once you have your copy dialed in, another way to attract your ideal recurring supporter is to partner with values-aligned brands.

FIND YOUR VALUES-ALIGNED PARTNERS

What corporate partners have you worked with over the years? Who's sponsored a table at a luncheon? This is the time to break out that list and cultivate a different type of partnership to raise awareness and recurring revenue.

In the nonprofit world, partnerships are more than just a line item on your annual report—they're a lifeline to sustainability and growth. Over the years, you've likely collaborated with various corporate partners, securing sponsorships for events, receiving in-kind donations, and building relationships that benefit both parties. But have you ever considered the untapped potential of values-aligned partnerships to elevate your organization's profile, reach new audiences, and grow your monthly donor base?

Partnerships go beyond transactional relationships.

They are rooted in shared missions and mutual goals, creating a synergy that amplifies the impact of both the nonprofit and the corporate partner. When a company's values align with your mission, it becomes more than just a sponsor; it becomes an advocate, a champion, and a valuable ally in your journey to create positive change.

In this section, we'll explore the importance of these partnerships and examples of win-win relationships and how they can be leveraged to increase your nonprofit's visibility, attract new donors, and ensure steady, reliable funding.

Take a moment to reflect on the corporate partners you've previously engaged with. Make a list here of who they are and how you've partnered in the past:

_____

_____

_____

_____

_____

_____

Perhaps they've sponsored a table at your annual luncheon, provided volunteers for your events, or even donated products for your fundraisers. These partners already believe in your cause to some extent. Now, imagine deepening those relationships by looping them into the vision of your monthly donor program and how they can play an important role.

This means engaging in meaningful conversations about how you can collaborate in ways that benefit both parties and make a tangible difference in the community.

Start with easy asks:

➡ Facilitate a lunch and learn for their employees and end with a call to action to give to your monthly giving program.

➡ Ask if they have a corporate matching opportunity for monthly gifts.

➡ Will they share a blurb about your mission in their internal/external newsletters or social posts?

I also want you to think about organizations you'd love to work with!

What local, national, global, trade organizations, or groups align with the mission you're trying to achieve?

Make a list here:

_____

_____

_____

_____

_____

_____

Pro Tip: Search LinkedIn for a marketing contact at the organizations above to connect with. Outside of corporate social responsibility (CSR) personnel, marketing has more budget and is always looking for creative ways to shine a positive light on the brand.

Once you find a contact, keep your outreach simple and clear on how this would be a win-win-win.

A win for your audiences.

A win for you.

A win for them.

I love real-world examples, so when I was planning my virtual Monthly Giving Summit I realized it would fall on #NationalCheesePizzaDay, so I HAD to make sure pizza was involved!

Why not reach out to Dominos?!

Here's a LinkedIn message I sent to their Chief Digital Officer:

Hey (NAME) - Thanks so much for connecting! I have a virtual summit I'm planning on 9/5 which also happens to be #nationalcheesepizzaday and thought there could be a fun brand partnership collaboration between Domino's and my attendees. :)

Would love to share more about the event and brainstorm some ideas.

Do you know who the best person would be to connect with on your team?

**the summit is for nonprofit professionals that have monthly giving programs

Sure enough, I got a response back with the contact information of the best team member to speak with.

When you're able to get on the phone to discuss the partnership, there's already interest from their end to make the time. You BOTH have assets that benefit each other.

Share the vision of the program and then dive into questions to learn about them:

1. What are the business goals for the next quarter or rest of the year?
2. What's your marketing focus?
    Any upcoming campaigns?

3. What does internal employee engagement
    look like?
4. What's a current challenge?

As they're talking, think about where you can be a good partner brainstorming solutions and ideas.

And then when they're asking you similar questions, be transparent about where you're having challenges and where you shine!

Let's look at a few examples of nonprofit x for-profit brand partnerships that are just genius!

IKEA X UNHCR

When I first saw IKEA and UNHCR (United Nations High Commissioner for Refugees) launched a significant partnership. I thought, "huh?"

But, wait... this is so smart and makes perfect sense.

The partnership started in 2010 when IKEA Foundation, the philanthropic arm of IKEA, initiated a collaboration with UNHCR to explore how they could contribute to improving living conditions for refugees.

What is IKEA great at? They are known for simply designed home products that are "easy" to put together.

UNHCR, on the flip side, offers assistance to refugees globally and can make use of IKEA's proficiency in designing and producing to tackle particular obstacles in refugee settlements.

Their work together led to the development of the "Better Shelter" modular housing solution of flat-pack shelters that provide improved living conditions compared to tents. This partnership continues today, expanding to provide solar-powered lights and skills training programs to help refugees become more employable.

You might be thinking, "OK, I see the big win here for UNHCR, but what does IKEA get out of this partnership outside of doing good?" It's not a secret that consumers like to spend with socially conscious businesses and employees like to work with them.

The press around this partnership put IKEA in the spotlight as a socially responsible company with a commitment to making a positive impact on global issues. They've received recognition and awards for their humanitarian efforts, and their internal teams were inspired and motivated, leading to a stronger sense of purpose in their work.

Incredible, right!? IKEA wasn't just buying tables at an event; they went ALL-IN and developed a housing solution. Think big, share your vision, and you never know what ideas a partner might bring to the table.

Another company that leads with giving back is TOMS Shoes.

TOMS X SEVA FOUNDATION

I've been a fan of TOMS Shoes since their inception because of their "One for One" model. They were one of the first companies that had a social impact agenda ingrained into the DNA of the business. In 2011, they expanded outside the shoe business and into eyewear, following the same "One for One" model with glasses, where each sale of TOMS glasses would help restore sight to someone in need. This is also the year they partnered with the Seva Foundation. The Seva Foundation isn't as widely recognized as UNHCR, and this partnership *put them on the map* with the socially conscious TOMS consumers. The Seva Foundation focuses on preventing blindness and restoring sight worldwide.

The business alignment here is clear. For TOMS, they expanded their model to include eye care and diversified their social impact, broadening their consumer base. The partnership with the Seva Foundation made this possible for them.

Because of their partnership, they've provided eye care to 600,000 people globally and established care in regions such as Nepal, Guatemala, and Egypt.

> **MINDSET SHIFT:** Don't discount the impact YOU can create for the brands you partner with.

TACO BELL X BOYS & GIRLS CLUBS OF AMERICA

Back in 1992, an unlikely but powerful partnership between Taco Bell and the Boys & Girls Clubs of America (BGCA) began. It turned out to be a game changer for countless young people across the country. Their collaboration aimed to support education and career readiness, giving teens the tools they needed to succeed in school and beyond.

This partnership was anchored by the Taco Bell Foundation for Teens, which is all about helping young people reach their full potential. They provided grants, scholarships, and resources to make a real difference. One of the coolest things to come out of this partnership is the Graduate for Más program. This initiative encourages teens to commit to graduating high school and chasing their dreams. It offers mentorship, resources, and incentives to keep them motivated.

Brian Niccol, Taco Bell's Former CEO, explained the company's motivation, saying, "At Taco Bell, we believe in making a difference in the lives of young people. Through our work with the Boys & Girls Clubs of America, we are able to provide the support and resources necessary for teens to succeed."

Jim Clark, the President and CEO of BGCA, couldn't agree more. He noted, "Our partnership with Taco Bell has been instrumental in helping us reach more youth and provide them with the tools they need to excel. The Graduate for Más program, in particular, has inspired many teens to stay in school and pursue their goals."

The partnership has significantly boosted high school graduation rates among participating teens. By providing essential educational resources and support, Taco Bell and BGCA have helped many young people stay in school and plan for their futures.

All of these partnerships focus on brand alignment, long-term impact, and engagement and loyalty.

It's time to revisit conversations with past partners and start new ones to amplify what you're trying to accomplish with your monthly giving program.

Now, I get it—partnerships don't happen overnight. How can you call in die-hard believers without relying on external support?

In these next two case studies, you'll hear an example of how to activate your existing superfans and how to use digital marketing to find them.

ACTIVATE YOUR EXISTING SUPERFANS CASE STUDY:

QWOCMAP (Queer Women of Color Media Arts Project)

122 Monthly Donors | 72% Retention Rate YoY

Mission: They use film to shatter stereotypes and biases, reveal the lived truth of inequality, and build community around art and activism.

What if your donors put on an annual event that attracted new monthly supporters? And I mean ran the whole thing: invites, programming, and organizing the venue.

I was fortunate to connect with Kebo Drew, the Managing Director of QWOCMAP. When I asked Kebo how they grow their monthly donors, I had that awkward open-mouth shocked/semiconfused face when she told me about the Angel Brunch event.

"We just show up to it. Yes, it's donor-run, the program, the full event, selling the tickets, inviting people, everything."

She explained, "The only thing we provide is the landing page to host it. And we design customized graphics for them to send to the donors on the back end. The donors plan the whole thing. A committee of about six donors that are monthly donors. They invite their friends to brunch. It's around 50-100 people, and that's where people are invited to join as monthly donors."

A moment of pause for how AWESOME this is.

MINDSET SHIFT: The Angel Brunch is a perfect example of how you can get creative with fundraising and not just rely on traditional methods. Because the Angel Brunch is not organized by the organization itself, but by a committee of recurring donors, this allows the organization to have a fresh perspective and reach new supporters who may not have been previously engaged.

The Angel Brunch is more than just a fundraising event. It is an opportunity for donors to become more involved in the organization's mission and spread the word to their friends and acquaintances. This builds a strong sense of community and camaraderie. It also allows donors to showcase their talents and creativity, as they are responsible for programming and organizing the entire event.

The success of the Angel Brunch is a testament to the power of collaboration and the dedication of monthly donors. By involving them in the planning and execution of the event, the organization is not only able to expand its donor base but also build stronger relationships with existing donors. This event serves as a reminder that supporters are more than just financial contributors; they are also passionate advocates for the cause. It is a win-win situation for both the organization and its donors and a great example of thinking outside the box when it comes to fundraising.

If you don't have something like this established, Kebo recommends just asking. Ask a superfan of your organization and see if they'd be interested in setting something like this up!

Maybe it doesn't start with an event but a social media push to raise awareness for the program, and you activate your monthly giving community to post a certain video or image all on one day or week during a campaign.

Who could you ask?

_____

_____

_____

ATTRACT NEW SUPERFANS

Speaking of social media, in the second case study we'll explore digital advertising, one of the best and *cheapest* forms of advertising to significantly raise awareness and call in the right audience. Through Meta, aka Facebook and Instagram, you can run ads for website traffic, to increase video views, get donations…and to grow your email list through lead generation ads.

Lead generation ads are specifically designed to collect someone's email address usually in exchange for a free resource.

Here are a few examples of lead magnets my Grow My List Ads Challenge clients have created:

1. 10 Tips for Your First Live Theatre Visit
2. 6 Daily Skills to Improve Your Mental Health
3. Top Safety Tips for Solo Travel
4. 5 Literacy Books & Articles for Teachers

If you want to learn more about how to target your ideal donor and set up lead generation ads, head to positiveequation.com/book where I have a list of resources for you!

When you plan to launch a recurring giving program, whom are you sharing it with? Investing in growing your email list to find new believers and share this new initiative with is extremely important.

One organization that's done an exceptional job at lead generation is IJM UK, or International Justice Mission. They are at the forefront of fighting slavery and human trafficking globally. One of the key strategies in sustaining its mission is its monthly giving program called Freedom Partners.

CASE STUDY:

IJM UK: Freedom Partners

Approx 3,000 Monthly Donors | 99% Retention Rate

Mission: A global organization that protects people in poverty from slavery and violence.

As one of the world's largest international anti-slavery organizations, its mission is to work with authorities and partners to make justice unstoppable.

Dean Gillespie, heading up digital and mass marketing at IJM UK, shared that The Freedom Partners program isn't just about securing funds—it's about creating a movement. "To build a lasting movement to stop slavery and trafficking, mobilizing committed supporters is crucial," Dean explained. The idea is to connect donors to the cause deeply and personally, empowering them to feel like they are making a tangible difference.

To grow their base of Freedom Partners, IJM UK launched a groundbreaking lead generation campaign called Handraisers. This campaign was heavily focused on using Facebook ads to attract new supporters by utilizing thirty-six different targeted ad variants focused on specific issues, from online exploitation of children to violence against women.

The campaign's concept was simple yet powerful. Ads directed people to optimized landing pages where they could "raise their hand" and show their support by providing their email address. This sign-up process was designed to be seamless and engaging. "We saw an incredibly successful new supporter mobilization, increasing IJM UK's email support list by 71% (over 9,000) in just three months," he proudly shared. But the success didn't stop at email sign-ups.

What was truly surprising to Dean was the conversion rate of these new leads into monthly donors. "We saw more people sign up and become regular givers right on the page where they were directed after the ad," he noted. This immediate conversion defied traditional marketing theories, which typically advocate for a longer nurturing process through email journeys.

He also emphasized the importance of leading with a recurring giving ask. "You've got to lead with recurring because one-off donations, while helpful, don't provide the sustainability needed to drive long-term change," he emphasized. As we've discussed at length now, this strategy aligns perfectly with the subscription economy trend, where people are accustomed to regular payments for services they value.

The Handraisers campaign wasn't just a one-off effort but part of a larger strategic road map Dean had prepared a few years ago. This road map included three key pillars: getting real, getting direct, and getting relational. "We identified the need to invest in marketing orchestration platforms, a robust website donation program, and a powerful digital mobilization strategy," Dean explained. The digital mobilization strategy was particularly innovative. They utilized various tools and tactics to keep new supporters engaged and move them towards becoming Freedom Partners. After signing up, supporters received a series of personalized emails that included impact stories, quizzes, and opportunities to engage further.

One of the standout elements was a quiz around modern slavery, which not only educated the supporters but also reinforced their commitment to the cause. Dean shared some impressive metrics that underscored the campaign's success. "We saw a 20% increase in the total value of all our fundraising income over the last couple of years," he noted. This was particularly significant given the challenging economic environment, including the cost of living crisis in the UK.

To ensure the long-term retention of these new regular donors, IJM UK implemented several engagement strategies. They hosted digital webinars, provided regular updates on their work, and created opportunities for supporters to connect with IJM experts. "We worked really hard at reducing our churn rate, getting it just under 1% for a year," Dean highlighted. This high retention rate is a testament to the value and engagement IJM provides to its Freedom Partners.

The campaign's success led to broader organizational changes. Dean mentioned that the learnings from the Handraisers campaign influenced IJM UK's overall approach to digital fundraising and supporter engagement. "We started to optimize our email journey, moving from monthly to weekly communications with clear calls to action," Dean said. This shift not only increased engagement but also fostered a more active and involved donor base.

> **You've got to lead with recurring** because one-off donations, while helpful, don't provide the sustainability needed to drive long-term change.

Dean Gillespie
Head of Digital and Mass Marketing
IJM UK

Another innovative aspect of their strategy was the introduction of matched giving specifically for their regular giving program. This approach proved to be highly effective. "We saw a 140% increase in the value of new regular gifts during our most successful regular giving appeal," Dean shared.

The combination of digital strategies, matched giving, and personalized engagement created a powerful formula for growth. This movement mentality is at the core of IJM's mission, inspiring donors to see themselves as active participants in the fight for justice. IJM UK's Handraisers campaign demonstrates the power of strategic digital mobilization and recurring giving. By leveraging targeted Facebook ads, personalized engagement tactics, and a focus on sustainability, IJM UK was able to significantly grow its base of monthly donors and create a lasting impact in the fight against slavery and human trafficking.

Dean's creative approach and passionate commitment to the cause serve as a powerful example for others looking to build and sustain their own movements for change.

When you think about where your supporters are—I'd place a pretty heavy bet that they're one of the five billion monthly active users on Facebook and Instagram! And trust me—I know running ads can be intimidating and you don't want to spend money unsure of what your outcome will be. But this is where aligning on some sort of marketing strategy and budget from the beginning is important. Marketing is testing and seeing what works—and with social media ads you can do that and find your believers.

Leaning back on the words of Marcus Collins, "Where's your congregation?"

Do you have the messaging, the partners, the welcome email funnels, etc. to call in your believers? When you've found your crew, they'll not only show up every month, but when empowered to do so, they'll be the biggest champions and amplifiers of the mission.

AHA Moments!

1. **Harness the Power of Community:** The story of becoming a die-hard UCF Knights fan illustrates the power of community and shared experiences in building loyal supporters. Just like season ticket holders in college football, your monthly giving program should create a sense of belonging and identity, fostering a strong, dedicated community.

2. **Leverage Personal Stories:** Don't forget about telling your personal story here too. When posting on LinkedIn or hosting potential donors at an event, sharing your personal experiences with the mission, like traveling to mission sites, helps potential supporters connect emotionally with your cause. Highlighting personal journeys can inspire others to join and support your mission, creating a deeper connection.

3. **Empower Supporters to Fundraise Creatively:** Movember's success with creative fundraising challenges shows the importance of allowing supporters to take ownership. Encouraging your supporters to develop their unique fundraising ideas can lead to innovative and effective campaigns, enhancing engagement and participation.

4. **Focus on Clear, Inclusive Messaging:** Effective copywriting is essential for attracting and retaining supporters. Use simple, relatable language that speaks directly to your audience's values

and passions. Including supporters in the narrative, using "we" and "you," can make them feel like an integral part of your mission, fostering long-term loyalty.

5. **Grow Your Fan Base:** Running targeted ads on platforms like Facebook and Instagram can significantly expand your reach, driving traffic to your website, increasing video views, and growing your email list through lead generation ads. These ads collect email addresses by offering valuable resources, helping you build a strong base of supporters. An excellent example of this strategy is IJM UK's Handraisers campaign, which effectively used targeted Facebook ads to attract new supporters and convert them into monthly donors, demonstrating the power of strategic digital mobilization and recurring giving.

NEXT STEPS:

_____

_____

_____

_____

_____

_____

_____

_____

_____

_____

_____

"DO NOT PASS GO AND DO NOT COLLECT $200."

BEFORE WE DIVE into Step 4: Make the Ask, let's pause and heed the classic Monopoly advice: "Do not pass Go and do not collect $200."

Steps 1-3 are crucial to address before we move on to the fundraising stage. While I'm sure you're eager to bring in funds, it's essential to first establish a solid foundation for your product, optimize the giving experience, and craft compelling language to engage potential donors. Without these elements in place, you risk leaving money on the table.

Remember, everything doesn't have to be perfect to start, but a strong foundation is key to maximizing your success.

CHAPTER 9
Step 4: Make The Ask

WHEN YOU'RE ASKED by Netflix to pay $15.49 (or whatever the going rate is) for entertainment each month, do you question the monthly subscription or just dive into binging the latest *Bridgerton* or *Love is Blind*?

Every time you order from Amazon, do you remember you've paid an annual subscription for Amazon Prime or just get excited that in less than twenty-four hours you'll have a sun hat for your baby?

When your Nuuly clothing rental box shows up with seven items to wear, are you thinking about the $89 you pay each month or how you're not spending that on one shirt at Banana Republic?

And when I say you...I mean me because these are all subscriptions I have and never question!

They make my life easier and provide value. You probably feel the same way about that magazine, coffee, or food subscription you love.

Seems easy to wrap your mind around, right? The company markets you a service, you see the value and say yes.

Now, imagine asking your donors for a recurring gift with the same ease. Back to our money mindset—monthly giving isn't just about donations; it's about giving people a way to channel their purpose consistently.

MINDSET SHIFT: By framing monthly contributions as a purposeful commitment, you empower donors to support your mission regularly, creating a lasting impact together. Let's make the ask with confidence and flair because it's more than just money—it's a movement!

In this chapter, we're jumping into the best part!!

Drum roll please....the moment you've been waiting for.

You'll start seeing the return of your hard work by inviting people IN and asking for a transformational monthly gift. In this chapter, I'll share ideas to build the ask for different segments of your existing audience, new people, five growth case studies, and my perspective on a few top FAQs.

Since we live in an age of instant gratification, it's important to remember that growing a regular giving program takes time and consistent effort. You need to talk about it ALL the time to see real results.

> *It's easy to look at an organization that's been doing this for a decade and start to compare ourselves and get frustrated. Don't! YOU are on your own beautiful journey. And remember, the best part of being part of a mastermind is getting to hear from your peers on their learned experiences.*

Well, reader, YOU are in this Monthly Giving Mastermind.

Let's explore how to grow your monthly donors!

ALWAYS ON + TENTPOLE MOMENTS

If you don't ask, your program won't grow. Period.

One email campaign a year just won't cut it. You need to have an "always on" strategy and a "tentpole moments" strategy.

Always On Strategy

Think of this as keeping your monthly giving program in the spotlight all the time. Mention it everywhere—at fundraising events, in emails, text messages, podcast interviews, with partners, and on social media. The idea is that anyone who hears about your organization should immediately think of your monthly giving program.

Remember that one-liner we created earlier? Use it whenever someone asks, "What do you do?" Keeping this consistent message helps make your program memorable and clear.

Tentpole Moments Strategy

These are specific times, maybe two or three times a year, where you go all out to get new regular donors or encourage your existing supporters to up their contributions. You likely have big events or campaigns already in place—just make sure to center your recurring giving during these times.

You might feel like a broken record, but according to the "Rule of 7" in marketing, people need to see a message at least seven times before they take action. So, even if it feels repetitive, keep the story and call-to-action to become a monthly donor front and center.

With your existing audience, you might not need to hit the seven times mark, but staying consistent and engaging them regularly is still crucial to turning their interest into ongoing support.

EXPANDING THE ASK TO YOUR EXISTING AUDIENCE

It's time to comb through your existing supporters, segment them, and categorize into donor types. I recommend creating three different lists. You can go way more in-depth here depending on the data you track, but this is a good starting point:

1. One-time supporters
2. Lapsed donors
3. Never given

If you have the information, I'd go deeper to segment:

1. Most engaged email subscribers (every email platform is different, but I'd base this on open rates and click links)
2. Donated less than $100 multiple times over the past two years
3. Clicked on the donate button but haven't converted

Each of these audiences should receive a personalized email campaign (four to five emails) announcing your monthly giving program, telling impact stories, what you're working on that's timely and relevant, and how they can get involved.

Email is the primary channel for communication with supporters, so I'm focusing here first; plus, you can take long-form content like an email and repurpose it for other channels.

Email is key but as you've heard time and time again, you need to communicate where your supporters are. This means an omni-channel approach. Choose the channels you can manage well, whether it's SMS, social media, events, podcasts, or others.

OTHER CHANNELS AND IDEAS:
1. **SMS**: Send timely impact updates and reminders to join the monthly giving program.
2. **Social Media**: Post engaging story content and success stories to reach a broader audience. Make sure you're always providing the appropriate call-to-action based on the platform directing people to your landing page. (Ex. On Instagram, you'd use "link in bio" language versus on Facebook you can directly post the link within the text.)

3. **Paid Social**: Run targeted ads to attract new donors.

4. **Events**: Make your monthly giving program the focus at fundraising events.

5. **Speaking Engagements**: Discuss the benefits, impact, and how people can give monthly during public speaking opportunities.

6. **Podcasts**: Feature interviews with beneficiaries and supporters.

7. **Connected TV Advertising**: CTV advertising is a new way for nonprofits to reach potential donors through streaming TV services. These are ads on the Hulu's of the world to target specific audiences based on set demographics and interests, to reach people who are more likely to be interested in your cause and potentially become donors.

8. **Experiential Marketing**: Create memorable in real life "IRL" experiences that highlight your cause.

9. **Thought Leadership**: Write LinkedIn posts, articles, and blogs showcasing your expertise and mission.

10. **Partners**: Collaborate with other organizations to expand your reach.

Circle the ones you think you want to start with!

Expand on ideas for each here:

_____

_____

_____

_____

_____

_____

And speaking of doing things a bit different when it comes to asking…when you're looking to start a new monthly giving program and convert one-time supporters to recurring, consider an invite-only launch.

How would this work?

MINDSET SHIFT: An Invite-Only Launch

Instead of opening it to everyone right away, you make it an invite-only event. Your current supporters and peers get special referral links to invite their friends and family. This approach not only creates buzz but also fosters a sense of exclusivity and community among your donors—turning them into superfans!

Let's explore how this strategy has worked for other successful companies and how you can make it work for your cause.

An invite-only launch leverages the power of personal connections. When your existing supporters invite their network, it adds a layer of trust and credibility. Plus, it makes people feel special and gives you the ability to test what works before reaching out to a wider audience.

WHAT DOES THIS LOOK LIKE IN PRACTICE?

MoviePass: MoviePass started as a subscription-based movie ticket service, offering users the ability to watch multiple movies per month for a flat fee. Initially, MoviePass used an invite-only model to create a sense of exclusivity and curiosity. Early adopters shared their experiences, creating a buzz that rapidly increased its popularity. The model was particularly appealing because it disrupted the traditional way people accessed movies, making it more affordable and convenient. Despite later operational and financial challenges, MoviePass's initial invite-only approach played a crucial role in its rapid growth and media attention.

Soho House: Soho House is a private members' club known for its exclusivity and high-profile clientele. Established in London in 1995, it has expanded globally, maintaining a selective membership process. Prospective members need a referral from an existing member and must undergo a selection process. This exclusivity has built a prestigious brand image, attracting creatives and professionals from various industries. The allure of being part of a selective community has contributed to Soho House's enduring appeal and the loyalty of its members. Membership grants access to beautifully designed spaces, exclusive events, and a network of influential people.

Facebook: Think back to Facebook's early days. Initially, it was only open to Harvard students, then to other Ivy League schools, and eventually to all universities. The need for a .edu email address made it feel exclusive, driving demand and growth through word-of-mouth. This strategy created a sense of community and exclusivity, making students eager to join. It wasn't just about connecting online; it was about being part of a digital revolution that everyone wanted in on.

BRINGING THIS STRATEGY TO YOUR NONPROFIT

1. **Mobilize Your Current Supporters** Start with your loyal donors and volunteers. Give them personalized referral links and encourage them to invite friends and family. Highlight how their referrals can significantly expand your mission's reach.

2. **Emphasize Exclusivity** Frame the invite-only launch as a unique opportunity to be the first to join your monthly giving community. Offer early members special perks like exclusive updates, events, or recognition to make them feel valued.

3. **Share Impact Stories** Illustrate the potential impact of the program with compelling stories. For example, "By inviting just five friends to join, you can help provide clean water to an entire village for a year." Use visuals and testimonials to show the difference their referrals can make.

4. **Track and Celebrate Referrals** Set up a system to track referrals and recognize top referrers. Maybe create a leaderboard

or offer small rewards for those who bring in the most new supporters. Ask your donation platform if they have something like this available. Platforms that generate unique referral links for each supporter and provide real-time updates on their progress can be incredibly helpful. Public recognition can keep the excitement going!

5. **Engage New Members** Once new members join, make sure they feel welcomed. Send personalized welcome messages, provide program updates, and offer ways for them to engage more deeply with your cause.

Implementing an invite-only launch for your monthly giving program can create excitement and a sense of belonging. Inspired by successful examples from the business world, this strategy can help you build a dedicated community of supporters who are passionate about your mission. So, why not give it a try? Your superfans are out there, ready to spread the word and make a difference!

When it comes to inviting new people in, I have five case studies to share with you with five very different approaches on how they've grown their monthly giving programs.

Get cozy, grab a beverage, and get ready to be inspired!

GROWTH CASE STUDIES

charity: water—The Spring

60,000+ Monthly Donors | 98% Retention Rate

Mission: Bringing clean and safe water to people around the world.

When I shared the importance of video in Step 2: Make It Easy, I teased charity: water's infamous compelling twenty-minute documentary, *The Spring*. It launched on Facebook and YouTube to celebrate their decade-long journey and set the stage for introducing their monthly giving program, The Spring. But what's the back story? How did this program we all look up to first begin?

Let's go back to August 2016.

charity: water launched The Spring, designed to create a sustainable revenue stream and engage donors in a deeper, ongoing relationship with their mission. The initiative was a strategic move for the organization, aiming to build a steady and predictable source of funding to support their clean water projects around the world.

Cubby Graham, discussing the genesis of The Spring, explained that the idea stemmed from the need to address the organization's annual financial reset. "January 1st would come around, and we would start at zero every year," Graham noted. charity: water's model initially relied heavily on fundraising campaigns and individual events like birthday donations. However, this approach lacked the consistency needed for long-term planning and sustainability.

They recognized the success of other nonprofits' monthly giving programs, typically characterized by a one-to-one sponsorship model. However, they faced a unique challenge: their work involved funding large-scale water infrastructure projects rather than individual sponsorships. This made it difficult to create a direct, personal connection between donors and beneficiaries. "We couldn't create that one-to-one relationship with the donor and the person that they're impacting," Graham explained. Instead, they aimed to foster a sense of collective impact and community among their supporters.

The launch of The Spring was marked by a twenty-minute documentary film of the same name, celebrating charity: water's ten-year anniversary. The film played a crucial role in the program's success, as it provided a comprehensive overview of the organization's journey, milestones, and future goals. "We launched the program with a documentary called *The Spring*...to hold a moment to just celebrate," Graham said. Despite initial skepticism about the length of the film in the age of short attention spans, it performed exceptionally well on platforms like Facebook and YouTube, driving significant engagement and conversions.

This in-depth storytelling approach allowed viewers to connect deeply with the organization, far more effectively than shorter ads. By immersing potential donors in the mission and milestones of charity: water, the film successfully drove significant interest and commitment to the program.

The initial response to *The Spring* surpassed expectations, thanks in large part to the powerful storytelling in the film. "The film certainly still converts... by the end of it, they feel like they've gotten to know the organization so much more," Graham noted. This deep connection was crucial, as it helped potential donors understand and commit to the recurring nature of their contributions.

He shared that there was another initial version of the video that opened with fifteen seconds or so of slow-motion water footage, very Nat Geo like, very cinematic, and people weren't interested. They were dropping off early. It wasn't until those first fifteen seconds were cut and the video dropped people immediately into founder Scott Harrison's story that things really took off. This adjustment is a testament to the importance of paying attention to data and making changes when needed.

Promotion of The Spring didn't stop with the film. They integrated the program into their broader communication strategy, discussing it at events, through social media, and in email campaigns. "We shifted a lot of our comms and focus on growing The Spring," Graham said, emphasizing the importance of regular updates and exclusive content to keep donors engaged. This approach ensured that donors felt continuously connected to the impact of their contributions.

The management of The Spring is an all-hands-on-deck effort. Currently, the primary responsibility lies with the email team, supported by a lifetime value squad, engineers, and copywriters. This collaborative approach ensures that all communications are consistent, engaging, and impactful. The program thrives on delivering regular, inspiring content to its members, mirroring the subscription models of popular services like Spotify and Netflix.

"We're following the whole country program... they're getting exclusive Sierra Leone content all year long," Graham mentioned, illustrating the organization's commitment to transparency and donor engagement.

Looking forward, Cubby emphasizes the critical role of content in engaging monthly donors.

"I think content and stories are like the bread and butter of our monthly giving program...people subscribe to Spotify for music and Netflix for content... they want to be inspired." Subscribers expect regular, quality updates, similar to other subscription services. charity: water focuses on producing exclusive content—videos, films, and photos—that keep their community inspired and connected to the impact of their contributions. This content-driven approach is central to the sustained growth and success of The Spring.

MINDSET SHIFT: You might think this major emphasis on monthly giving might alienate major donors. Instead, as charity: water found with The Spring, monthly giving serves as a bridge to larger gifts.

The program allows donors who might face financial constraints in a given year to spread their contributions over twelve months. Additionally, high-capacity donors often start with significant monthly gifts, such as $500 per month, which can lead to major donor status. The ongoing relationship and regular updates provided through The Spring nurture these connections, often resulting in larger, one-time gifts or project sponsorships.

The Spring is known as one of the most successful monthly giving programs out there with their ever-growing supporter base and strong retention rate. It started with going against the grain with a twenty-minute documentary when we're all taught to create short, sharable content. Disruptive and different content stands out!

Here are five takeaways from charity: water to think about within your own program:

1. **Embrace Compelling Storytelling**: Like charity: water's 20-minute documentary, use in-depth storytelling to connect deeply with potential donors and drive engagement.

2. **Use Data to Refine Your Approach**: Be ready to adjust your strategies based on data and feedback, just as charity: water did with their film.

3. **Integrate Across Channels**: Promote your program through multiple channels and ensure consistent, engaging communication to keep donors connected.

4. **Bridge to Larger Gifts**: Use monthly giving as a stepping stone to major gifts by nurturing ongoing relationships and providing regular updates.

5. **Focus on Consistent, Quality Content**: Regular, inspiring content is key to retaining donors and making them feel connected to your mission.

In this next example, Because International had an existing recurring giving program but decided it needed a rebrand. As your mission and culture evolves over time, you might find yourself in need of a refresh as well. Here's a great example of how they utilized this rebrand moment to grow their monthly donors.

Because International: The Sole

211 Monthly Donors | 81% Retention Rate

Mission: To alleviate poverty by distributing impact products and supporting product-focused entrepreneurs.

In late 2020, Because International found themselves at a pivotal moment. The nonprofit, known for their innovative product The Shoe That Grows, decided to rebrand its existing monthly giving program, Footprints, into a more focused and impactful initiative called The Sole. This rebranding was not merely a name change; it was a strategic move to enhance their outreach and distribution efforts, especially as the pandemic presented new challenges.

The timing of the rebranding was crucial. By launching The Sole during the Christmas season, Because International leveraged the inherent generosity of the holiday period (a tentpole moment). This strategic timing was designed to maximize engagement and capitalize on the philanthropic spirit that flourishes during the holidays.

To spread word about The Sole, Because International deployed a comprehensive multichannel campaign. They targeted their existing supporter base through a series of email and social media campaigns, ensuring that their loyal donors were the first to hear about the new initiative. These efforts paid off! The initial response was overwhelmingly positive, with the number of monthly donors increasing significantly. "Through those efforts, we saw a pretty big boost just in the first few months on top of what had been in Footprints previously, as well as some pretty good system growth for us in that first year," Hannah Braly, Communications Specialist, added.

By the end of 2021, The Sole had grown from eighty-six to 212 members. However, the team at Because International knew that initial growth was only part of the equation. Retaining these new members was equally important.

They focused on personalized communication, sending new members emails and tangible acknowledgments like cards and stickers to foster a sense of belonging and appreciation, made possible in part by having a team member dedicated to retention communication. "Our retention rate has gotten better, and we are holding onto people a little bit better than we were originally, which I think is probably due to having a dedicated team member," Linnea Thomas, Director of Marketing, explained. This attention to retention helped solidify the gains made during the Christmas campaign. Looking forward, Because International has set ambitious goals for The Sole.

They aim to have a thousand members by the end of 2025. "We'd like to have a thousand members by the end of next year, the end of 2025, which is pretty aggressive. And we feel optimistic about it," Thomas said, underscoring their commitment to growth and sustainability.

Because International's rebranding of Footprints to The Sole, strategically timed around a tentpole moment (the holiday season), and executed through a well-rounded multichannel campaign, has set a solid foundation for future growth. Their focus on personalized engagement and retention has ensured that their initial successes are sustainable, positioning them well for achieving their ambitious membership goals.

If you have an existing program that's not growing at the rate you'd like, could it be time for a refresh? Does it align with who you are *now* versus when it was created?

Consider these five takeaways as you assess your program:

1. **Strategic Tentpole Timing**: Launching The Sole during the Christmas season maximized engagement by tapping into the holiday giving spirit.
2. **Multichannel Campaign**: A combination of email campaigns, ads, and social media effectively spread the word and boosted donor numbers.

3. **Personalized Communication**: Sending emails, cards, and stickers to new members fostered a sense of belonging and improved retention rates.

4. **Dedicated Team**: Having a dedicated team member focused on retention helped maintain and solidify initial growth.

5. **Ambitious Goals**: Setting clear, ambitious goals for future growth demonstrates commitment to sustainability and long-term impact.

If you're not in refresh mode, but at the beginning and looking to do a bold launch, what kind of campaign would align with the goal of the monthly giving community and rally them to take action? In this next example, you'll meet The Adventure Project and learn how one campaign generated one hundred new monthly donors!

The Adventure Project: The Collective

383 Monthly Donors | 88% Retention Rate

Mission: Creates jobs to empower communities to work their own way out of extreme poverty, for good.

I've been a big fan of Becky Straw, co-founder of The Adventure Project, for years and was fortunate to work with them on a recent campaign. At the time, they ran a lean and mighty team of two full-time people and are proof of what's possible with a small team. The Collective, their monthly giving program, was suggested by her co-founder, Jodi Landers, during their organization's first year, a time when they were working without salaries to prove their model and find a product-market fit. The initial goal was modest: to get fifty to one hundred people to support their operations monthly. However, they quickly realized the potential for a broader community as grassroots givers expressed a preference for a "set it and forget it" model, allowing them to contribute regularly without being repeatedly solicited. This demand led to the creation of The Collective.

Becky explained, "A lot of our grassroots givers were just saying, 'I love all the programs you do. Can I just join monthly?'" The name "The Collective" was chosen to reflect the idea that small contributions, when pooled together, can create significant impact. "It doesn't take much to create impact, but collectively together we do a lot," she said.

This collective effort has allowed The Adventure Project to leverage approximately $20,000 monthly to drive change in Africa. The Collective was launched with another strategic tentpole moment, a Labor Day campaign where they distributed "You're Hired" cards to their Founder Circle members and encouraged them to share these on social media, inviting friends and family to join the program. This campaign proved to be highly effective, resulting in one hundred new monthly donors.

Over the years, growth and adoption of The Collective has continued, primarily driven by referrals and email marketing. A key strategy has been to focus on increasing the contributions of existing donors rather than solely acquiring new ones. She highlighted, "We've actually seen our biggest lift revenue-wise from people increasing their gift versus just trying to figure out how to find new people."

Maintaining donor engagement and retention has been a challenge, particularly during periods when the organization's focus shifts to major givers. Despite these challenges, The Collective has remained a consistent source of revenue. Becky emphasized the importance of this stability, stating, "We're still getting consistent revenue, consistent engagement, even though we've had to press pause on funneling people through."

Personalization and authenticity have been critical in their communication strategy.

New members receive personalized emails and handwritten cards. While automated email campaigns are a goal, they currently rely on these personal touches to build connections with their donors. "The more that we can send emails that are personalized, the more likely we're getting people to click through," Straw noted.

Matching gifts from other donors or corporations have also been an effective strategy for increasing donations. "Any amount that you increase your gift will be matched," Straw shared, explaining that this approach has been more effective than offering physical incentives like t-shirts. Looking to the future, she believes that monthly giving will become a core focus for most nonprofits, given its scalability and the ability to forecast revenue more accurately.

She observed, "Most nonprofits are going to start making this one of their core focus areas because it's just the way that people prefer to give." Reflecting on their journey, Becky

> **We've actually seen our biggest lift revenue-wise from people increasing their gift** versus just trying to figure out how to find new people.

Becky Straw
Co-founder
The Adventure Project

expressed a common sentiment: "If I could go back in time, I would have started sooner."

The success of The Collective demonstrates the power of community and consistent engagement in driving sustained support for nonprofit initiatives. Through strategic campaigns, personalized communication, and leveraging matching gifts, The Adventure Project has built a robust monthly giving program that continues to grow and support its mission.

As you brainstorm a new campaign or initial launch, lean on the learnings here from The Adventure Project:

1. **Grassroots Demand**: The Collective was created in response to donor preferences for a "set it and forget it" giving model.
2. **Strategic Naming**: The name reflects the power of small, collective contributions to create significant impact.
3. **Focus on Existing Donors**: Increasing contributions from current donors has driven revenue growth more than acquiring new donors.
4. **Personalized Communication**: Personalized emails and handwritten cards enhance donor engagement and retention.
5. **Matching Gifts**: Offering donation matching has been more effective than physical incentives.

Are you in a stage ready to scale? You've had good success with organic efforts but really want to take your brand awareness and growth to the next level. Get ready to be blown away by Kyle Roosen's digital ads strategy at the Tim Tebow Foundation.

Tim Tebow Foundation: The Defenders / The Movement

20,000 Monthly Donors | 90% Retention Rate

Mission: To bring Faith, Hope, and Love to those needing a brighter day in their darkest hour of need.

Kyle Roosen, Senior Director of Marketing at the Tim Tebow Foundation (TTF), shared the evolution and impressive growth of their monthly donor programs through the strategic use of paid social ads. Initially, TTF's monthly giving program was quite simple, featuring a toggle on-off on their standard donation page. Roosen, who joined TTF in December 2014, sought to innovate and create something more engaging.

In 2016, inspired by successful programs like charity: water's The Spring and Pencils of Promise's Passport, Roosen launched The Movement. This program was designed as a branded monthly donor community, allowing donors to feel they were part of something significant. Initially launched via email, The Movement attracted about 225 members at an average of $30 per month.

Despite this promising start, growth plateaued around $800,000 to $900,000 annually from 2016 until 2020. Roosen noted, "We were losing donors as fast as we were gaining them due to issues like credit card fraud and failing transactions." This led them to switch technology platforms from Classy to Blackbaud and Luminate, although this move was not successful, and they ended up switching back to Classy as the

THE MONTHLY GIVING MASTERMIND   211

product improved. A nod here to knowing when a platform is limiting you from reaching your potential or doesn't have the functionality you need to scale.

In 2020, TTF publicly launched its anti-human trafficking ministry, prompting the creation of the Defenders program, a second monthly giving initiative focused on this cause. With an initial minimum donation of $40, the Defenders program was tailored for those passionate about combating human trafficking. Roosen explained, "We built an email list of 20,000 people who wanted to be the first to know about the launch, capturing excitement and momentum." A pivotal change came in the summer of 2023 when Roosen took over Facebook ad management. What started as a few hundred dollar test turned into a key strategy for acquisition. "Since last June, I've spent almost a million dollars on Facebook ads and have returned about $3.7 million," Roosen stated.

This significant investment in ads saw their monthly donor base grow from 6,500 to 18,000 in less than a year, with annual revenue from these programs now at $10.4 million. The ads, while primarily focused on recurring donations, also attracted one-time gifts. Roosen shared, "The call to action is very much recurring, but we get people that toggle the monthly giving option off on the donation page." Their success with ads was partly due to leveraging Facebook's algorithm with little to no audience targeting, allowing the platform to optimize ad delivery on its own.

Another key component of their ad strategy was using compelling video content. A particularly successful video from

2020, telling the story of a trafficking survivor and featuring Tim Tebow, has consistently performed well, bringing in significant donations. "I've been running it since July, and it just keeps going," Roosen remarked.

PAUSE.

A video from 2020 is still performing and being used now. Just wanted to make sure you caught that.

MINDSET SHIFT: When we post something once, we think it's done. Finito. "Everyone saw it." This is proof that dialing in and repurposing content that works has legs...for years!

Retention and donor experience are also crucial for TTF. Despite a churn rate of 2-4%, with some donors mistakenly signing up for monthly donations, TTF focuses on consistent storytelling and acknowledging donors' contributions. Roosen described their process: "First touchpoint is the receipt, second is an automatic welcome email, then they get a story or their t-shirt, and we're building a 12-month experience to celebrate milestones." TTF's growth strategy also includes leveraging technology like Classy's pop-up feature, which asks one-time donors to switch to monthly donations, a tactic that increased conversion rates significantly.

Reflecting on their journey, Roosen highlighted the importance of focusing on both acquisition and retention. He expressed a desire to have brought in an Experience Manager sooner to balance these efforts. Looking ahead, TTF plans to launch another monthly initiative engaging donors more deeply with specific missions worldwide.

Roosen's advice for other nonprofits looking to grow their monthly donor programs is clear: "It doesn't matter how great your monthly giving program is if you don't have anyone to talk to. First and foremost, build your audience consistently, and then offer them compelling opportunities to be part of your mission."

Through innovative strategies, significant testing and investment in digital advertising, and a focus on donor experience, the Tim Tebow Foundation has successfully transformed its monthly donor programs to be approximately 33% of their annual revenue, setting a powerful example for other nonprofits of what's possible.

If you've historically been adverse to spending money on advertising, this is an incredible testament to the reach and action they can create. As someone who teaches Meta advertising, I strongly recommend hiring someone qualified to get you started. If one ad doesn't work great, that's OK! It's all a learning process.

They're one of the cheapest ads to purchase, but they do require a budget for testing. What copy, graphics, and audiences will perform best? You have to be OK to spend a little to gain learnings and with TTF, they went through that process and ended up with a winning result!

Build your audience consistently, and then offer them compelling opportunities to be part of your mission.

Kyle Roosen
Senior Director of Marketing
Tim Tebow Foundation

Ready to scale? What actions items can you take away from TTF?

1. **Email List Utilization**: Building and leveraging an email list of 20,000 interested individuals for the Defenders program demonstrates the power of email marketing. By creating anticipation and excitement before the launch, TTF was able to capture significant momentum and donor engagement.

2. **Significant Ad Investment**: Roosen's strategic investment in Facebook ads—spending nearly $1 million and returning about $3.7 million—highlights the potential of paid social advertising. This approach significantly expanded their donor base and showcases the effectiveness of allocating substantial resources to digital marketing when done correctly.

3. **Video Content**: The use of compelling video content, such as a powerful video from 2020 featuring Tim Tebow and a trafficking survivor, has been crucial. This video not only performed well initially but continues to drive donations years later, emphasizing the lasting impact of high-quality storytelling.

4. **Audience Building**: Roosen's advice to other nonprofits— "First and foremost, build your audience consistently, and then offer them compelling opportunities to be part of your mission"—stresses the importance of audience development. Building a dedicated and engaged audience is foundational to the success of any donor program.

5. **Matching Gifts and Minimal Targeting**: Utilizing matching gift campaigns and leveraging Facebook's algorithm with minimal targeting have proven to be effective strategies. Matching gifts increase donor contributions, while minimal targeting allows Facebook's algorithm to optimize ad delivery, improving campaign performance.

Do you serve a more regional or local audience? You could be the perfect candidate to try face-to-face canvassing. In the following case study, Feeding Westchester shares how they implemented this approach for recurring giving.

Feeding Westchester: Nourishing Neighbors

2,200 Monthly Donors | 76%—face-to-face channel, 91% Retention for other channels

Mission: To nourish our neighbors in the fight against hunger. We envision a community where all people have access to the food they need today and the fundamental resources to build a better tomorrow.

Brittany Frieder, Manager of Donor Relations, discussed the remarkable growth of Feeding Westchester's monthly donor program, Nourishing Neighbors, driven by face-to-face efforts at a local level and strategic leadership buy-in. This comprehensive approach, along with focused investment in people and innovative fundraising techniques, has significantly expanded their recurring donor base.

Feeding Westchester employs a firm to carry out canvassing throughout Westchester County. Brittany explained, "We use a third-party firm that represents our organization in local malls, farmers' markets, and stores." This method has proven effective in engaging the community directly, leveraging the local appeal of Feeding Westchester. "People like to talk about their community and what's needed locally, which makes our approach more effective than that of national organizations," Brittany noted.

Yes, you heard that right.

Those people who stand outside your local Trader Joe's or CVS often asking for support for national or international causes can work even if your cause is hyperlocal. The success of their face-to-face initiative is significantly attributed to strategic investment and strong leadership support. Brittany emphasized, "We were able to make this investment due to some extra money found in the budget and the new VP's focus on growing our sustainer group." The third-party firm operates on a performance-based model, where their payment is tied to achieving a set number of donors. Brittany highlighted, "If they do not meet the mutually agreed-upon donor numbers, the charity is not responsible for paying the full fee."

A notable aspect of their strategy includes investing in marketing to attract new donors. Brittany shared, "Our new VP of development, with a background from Save the Children, wanted to split the budget more evenly to focus not just on one-time gifts but also on recurring gifts." This shift in budget allocation has led to increased one-time and recurring donations, showing the impact of targeted marketing efforts.

Within four months of starting the canvassing effort, Feeding Westchester has successfully signed up 450 new donors.

She acknowledged that while retention for face-to-face acquired donors can be lower than other methods, their current retention is trending higher, around 75%, due to their local, less competitive environment. "Our retention is higher because we're in a small, non-national market without the competition seen in places like New York City," she explained. The program targets sustaining donors, with a notable portion skewing older. Brittany observed, "The people that engage with me do skew older, though we've seen more younger donors recently through face-to-face efforts, particularly those in their early 20s."

She also noted that face-to-face canvassing often encourages quarterly and annual recurring donations, which have higher retention rates. Feeding Westchester has also explored other fundraising techniques like telemarketing. Brittany explained, "Telemarketing is another huge monthly giving tactic, and we target individuals who have given at least two gifts in the last year." This approach has been effective in converting warm leads into recurring donors. Investing in dedicated staff for the monthly giving program has been crucial. Brittany emphasized, "Having a specific person to focus on stewardship, such as sending holiday cards and handwritten thank-you notes, has been key to retaining donors."

These personalized touches make donors feel valued and appreciated, contributing to higher retention rates. The organization also uses digital tools like Fundraise Up for donation processing and Razor's Edge for CRM. However, tracking and

> **Having a specific person to focus on stewardship,** such as sending holiday cards and handwritten thank-you notes, has been key to retaining donors.

Brittany Frieder
Manager of Donor Relations
Feeding Westchester

integrating data across platforms remains a challenge. Brittany noted, "Tracking lifetime value and retention in Razor's Edge can be tricky, especially when donors switch from monthly to annual giving." As the program evolves, Brittany aims to implement anniversary cards and other touchpoints to further enhance the donor experience.

Reflecting on their journey, she stated, "If we could go back in time, we would have started sooner and understood the value of these donors much earlier." Her advice to other nonprofits is to invest in building resilient donor pipelines and to recognize the importance of sustainers in ensuring financial stability.

Feeding Westchester's success with Nourishing Neighbors highlights the power of community engagement, strategic investment, leadership support, and personalized stewardship in building and retaining a loyal donor base.

If you're a hyperlocal organization—or even a national organization with a recognizable brand or missions that's top of mind—this case study is a great example of getting out into the community and testing something new.

1. **Face-to-Face Acquisition Efforts:** To engage the community directly, employ a third-party firm to carry out canvassing efforts in local areas such as malls, farmers' markets, and stores. Consider employing a performance-based model involved in canvassing efforts. This ensures that payment is tied to achieving specific donor acquisition targets, minimizing financial risk for the nonprofit. If

the agreed-upon donor numbers are not met, the non-profit isn't responsible for paying the full fee, making it a cost-effective approach.

2. **Strategic Lead Generation:** During face-to-face efforts, how can you get people on the street to open up and share their story? If they're not ready to commit to give, can you invite them to sign a pledge? That way you collect their contact information and can reach out later.

3. **Leadership Buy-In:** Securing strategic investment from leadership is crucial. Nonprofits should work to gain buy-in from key leaders who can advocate for allocating budget towards growing the sustainer program. This might involve presenting data that illustrates the long-term benefits of a recurring donation model and how it can provide financial stability.

4. **Quarterly and Annual Recurring Donations:** Encouraging quarterly and annual recurring donations can improve retention rates. Nonprofits should provide flexible giving options that cater to donor preferences, ensuring they feel comfortable and committed to their chosen giving schedule.

5. **Continuous Improvement:** As the program evolves, adding additional touchpoints like anniversary cards can enhance the donor experience. Nonprofits should regularly evaluate and refine their engagement strategies to keep donors feeling connected and appreciated.

Woo! All of the case studies are great examples of how different and creative you can be making the ask to new and existing supporters.

Before jumping in the FAQs, I want to reiterate that you're on your own journey here.

The case studies shared here are meant to be thought starters for you in your brainstorming efforts of what might be applicable to where you're at. You got this!

Since the ask around monthly giving is such a hot topic, the next section addresses some of the most frequently asked questions I've received.

FAQs:

Q: ARE YOU SURE WE SHOULD ASK WITH A RECURRING-FIRST APPROACH?

A: Of your nonprofit's revenue streams, which one is the most sustainable and flexible? This is an important question that your nonprofit's management should be asking.

→ **Grants**—Can be unpredictable, often tied to specific projects, and subject to changes in funding priorities. This means that while they may provide a boost in revenue, they cannot be relied upon as a stable source of income.

→ **Events**—While potentially lucrative, are time-intensive and dependent on attendance and engagement, making them a volatile source of income. This means that even if you have a successful event, you may not be able to replicate that success in the future.

➤ **Major Donors and Corporate Partners**—Are vital but can be sporadic and dependent on economic fluctuations or organizational changes. This means that while they may provide a significant amount of revenue, it may not be consistent enough to sustain your nonprofit in the long term.

➤ **One-time Gifts**—Also sporadic and very difficult to reengage. In 2024, the average retention rate for one-time donors is 43%! This means that while one-time gifts may provide a boost in revenue, it is unlikely that those donors will continue to support your nonprofit in the future.

➤ **Peer-to-Peer**—A wonderful surge of donations, often new from family and friends supporting a participant, but not sustainable. This means that while peer-to-peer donations can be a great source of income, it is not a reliable source and should not be solely relied upon.

All of this to say, it's important to diversify your revenue streams, but with the average monthly giving retention rate at 80-90%, it should take priority in your marketing efforts. It's important to have multiple sources of income, and it is crucial to prioritize and focus on the most sustainable and reliable source, which is monthly giving. This will ensure that your nonprofit has a stable and consistent source of income to support its operations and programs.

Q: IS IT OK TO ASK A REGULAR DONOR FOR ANOTHER GIFT?

A: There's a very common fear or even anxiety that comes when asking someone for money, especially if they're already giving.

If someone's a monthly donor, should I ask them to give AGAIN?

During a recent Classy presentation, they mentioned 29% of one-time donors who became recurring did so in the first ninety days of giving! Meaning…don't wait to make that next ask!

Daily Giving wondered this as well and put it to the test when they created the Israel Emergency Fund initiated during a time of crisis. This fund was unique as it introduced a one-time payment option, a novelty for an organization primarily focused on recurring donations.

They discovered that a significant portion of the funds raised came from their regular contributors. "That nearly $500,000 raised is from 2,600 donations from 1,700 donors," Friedner shared. This indicated that about 10% of their recurring donor base was willing to give additional support during this critical time.

The success of the secondary ask was partly due to the established trust and engagement Daily Giving had with their donors. "Because we have a giving group of 15,000 accounts, 10% of them stood up and said we're ready to help in the time of need," Friedner noted. This highlights the importance of maintaining a strong relationship with donors, as it increases the likelihood of additional support when needed. Daily Giving plans to continue exploring secondary asks during key times.

Q: SHOULD I ASK MONTHLY DONORS TO INCREASE THEIR MONTHLY GIFT?

A: Yes. :) But not without providing constant updates on their impact first.

Here's why that matters…

I was a monthly donor to an organization for a year. I never received anything besides a monthly tax receipt email and at my one-year mark, they asked if I would increase my gift—I'm pretty sure there was a need to switch platforms too. I ended up canceling my monthly gift. And I never heard anything.

The team at The Water Project is an example of a program that excelled at knowing how to ask supporters to increase their gifts.

CASE STUDY:

The Water Project: The Water Promise Circle

907 Monthly Donors | 95% Retention

Mission: To unlock human potential by providing reliable water projects to communities in sub-Saharan Africa who suffer needlessly from a lack of access to clean water and proper sanitation.

The Water Promise Circle is a monthly giving program by The Water Project, and it has demonstrated impressive growth and retention since its inception. Courtney Feild, the Director of Marketing at The Water Project, provided an in-depth look at the program's journey from its launch to its current success, highlighting strategies that have proven effective in engaging and retaining donors.

Launched in 2012, The Water Promise Circle was conceived to support the maintenance of water projects. Initially, the organization used homegrown website tools and later integrated Recurly, an e-commerce platform, to facilitate recurring donations. The switch to Fundraise Up in early 2022 further streamlined the process, enhancing user experience and donor management.

The program started modestly with fifty members in 2012 but quickly gained traction. Courtney explained, "In those early years, it was doubling. So we were at 121 members in 2013 and 194 in 2014." This steady growth continued, with an annual increase of 100 to 150 new members. The initial launch strategy included integrating a monthly giving option on the website and sending out email announcements.

Water Promise members receive a tailored communication journey post-gift, starting with a monthly newsletter that provides updates and statistics on their contributions. They are excluded from all appeal campaigns except for holiday appeals. Depending on their level of involvement, members either have a donor representative reaching out every ninety days or receive "Notes from Courtney" every four to six weeks. These notes offer personal insights and impactful stories from ongoing projects, helping to keep donors connected and informed about the difference they are making.

The organization runs an annual New Year's campaign focused solely on monthly giving, boosting new subscriptions.

Digital advertising also plays a crucial role, with about 20% of the budget dedicated to promoting monthly giving. This includes Google AdWords and Bing ads, which have proven effective in attracting new donors. Many new donors opt for a monthly subscription as their first gift, indicating the success of these targeted ads. (Hello, #recurringfirst!)

Each year, existing donors are asked to increase their monthly contributions. Fundraise Up's automated tools facilitate this process, making it easy for donors to adjust their giving amounts. Courtney explained, "During our New Year's campaign, we ask current monthly donors to consider increasing their contributions. This is typically a 3-5% increase request, framed within the context of the ongoing need for sustainability and the growing impact their increased support can make." The messaging emphasizes how even a small increase can significantly enhance the organization's ability to maintain and repair water projects, ensuring continuous access to clean water for communities.

The 900+ members of The Water Promise Circle contribute significantly to the organization's sustainability efforts. The average monthly donation is $45, with the largest monthly gift being $5,000 and the smallest $10. The program's total annual contribution is approximately $500,000.

Another incredible example of an upsell campaign is from Chive Charities.

CASE STUDY:

Chive Charities: Green Ribbon Fund

*4,000 Monthly Donors | 98% Retention Rate

Mission: Dedicated to supporting underserved veterans, military families, first responders, and rare medical diagnosees with life-changing grants. Each week, they provide critical grants for individuals with life-altering or life-threatening needs.

In October of 2022, I interviewed Erika Carley, former Senior Director of Operations, on my podcast, *Missions to Movements*. Chive Charities has built a robust and impactful monthly donor program known as the Green Ribbon Fund, which has become the cornerstone of their fundraising efforts. Unlike many monthly giving programs, the Green Ribbon Fund launched on day one of Chive Charities' operations in 2012 and was designed to provide sustainable support for the organization's mission to assist veterans, first responders, military families, and individuals with rare medical conditions.

The fund supports a wide range of needs, including accessible vehicles, mobility devices, and therapies not covered by insurance. From its inception, the Green Ribbon Fund has been central to Chive Charities' financial stability, making up over 70% of their annual revenue. Once a year, Chive Charities runs a comprehensive donor acquisition campaign aimed at converting new monthly donors and engaging existing ones. The 2022 campaign, themed "Because of You," celebrated the organization's ten-year anniversary by highlighting a decade of impact and inviting supporters to help turn "no" into "yes" for deserving applicants.

The campaign kicked off with a heartfelt story written by the Executive Director, Brian Mercedes. This story was published on Chive Charities' website and detailed significant milestones and smaller, yet impactful moments from the past decade.

The narrative included a behind-the-scenes look at the organization's application review process, revealing the emotional and challenging decisions made to select grant recipients. This transparency and vulnerability aimed to foster a deeper connection with the audience. The campaign included segmented contact lists, value propositions, and follow-up messaging. Supporters who signed up for monthly giving or upgraded their donations received a commemorative challenge coin and were entered into raffles.

Existing monthly donors were invited to upgrade their giving levels or make additional one-time donations of $100 or more. This approach resulted in 695 donations, including 321 new monthly donors, 284 one-time donations, and ninety upgrades!

One key lesson from Chive Charities' experience is the importance of offering a range of giving levels. Initially, the program had only four levels, which limited its potential. Introducing higher levels, such as the Platinum Level for recurring giving at $200 and above, unlocked new opportunities for growth.

Within three months of launching this level, the organization gained 131 platinum-level donors, significantly boosting revenue. Looking ahead, Chive Charities aims to continue refining their strategies for major gifts while maintaining the high-touch, personalized approach that has made their monthly giving program so successful. Erika emphasizes the importance of inviting donors into the story and consistently demonstrating the impact of their support.

*At the time of my initial podcast recording, The Green Ribbon Fund had over 4,000 monthly donors with a retention rate of 98%, contributing significantly to Chive Charities' ability to plan and execute their mission.

I highlight all these stories to share there's so many different ways to get to your goal.

Not sure where you should start when it comes to your ask strategy? Scan QR here for my Monthly Giving Launch Checklist.

AHA Moments!

1. **Reframe Monthly Giving as a Purposeful Commitment:** Monthly giving should be positioned not just as a way to donate but as a meaningful, consistent commitment to the cause. By drawing parallels to everyday subscription services like Netflix or Amazon Prime, we emphasized the importance of presenting monthly donations as a value-driven, effortless way for donors to support a mission they care about. This mindset shift helps donors see their contributions as part of a larger movement, enhancing their sense of purpose and commitment.

2. **Effective Use of Storytelling and Transparency:** The success stories of various organizations, like charity: water and The Adventure Project, highlight the power of storytelling in monthly giving campaigns. Detailed narratives that include behind-the-scenes insights and personal stories of impact can deeply connect donors to the mission. Transparency about the organization's processes, challenges, and achievements fosters trust and engagement, encouraging sustained support from donors who feel a personal connection to the cause.

3. **Strategic and Comprehensive Campaign Planning:** Successful monthly giving programs involve well-thought-out, multi-channel campaigns that target both new and existing donors. Examples from Chive Charities and Because Inter-

national illustrate the importance of leveraging various platforms, from social media to email marketing, to reach potential donors. Offering incentives, such as commemorative items or exclusive content, can further motivate donors to commit to monthly contributions. Additionally, consistent and tailored follow-up communication is crucial for retention and engagement.

4. **Regular Donor Engagement and Upsell Opportunities:** Regular engagement with monthly donors through personalized communication, updates on impact, and special campaigns to increase donations are vital for maintaining high retention rates. The Water Project's annual upsell campaign, which asks donors to increase their monthly contributions by 3-5%, is an example of how ongoing donor stewardship and clear communication about the impact of their increased support can lead to significant growth.

NEXT STEPS:

_____

_____

_____

_____

_____

_____

_____

_____

_____

CHAPTER 10
Step 5: Share Constant Joy & Gratitude

THERE'S ALWAYS AN emphasis in our sector—and pretty much every business, on growth. Finding someone new to buy or give. And yes, more people bring more money, more impact, more change. But what if we focused just as much *or more* on the "thank yous" than the "will yous?" What if we shifted our focus from constantly acquiring new supporters to retaining and nurturing the ones we already have?

Lowering the churn rate and increasing the retention of regular supporters would be a huge sigh of relief. It's easy to get caught up in the numbers and forget about the individual people behind them. At the end of the day, it's the loyal supporters who will make the biggest impact on your organization. They are the ones who have chosen to give regularly for a reason. They believe in your cause and want to be a part of it.

In this chapter, you'll hear the retention plans and tools utilized to maintain and further steward supporter relationships.

MINDSET SHIFT: So far, we've talked a lot about how to build a program that will cultivate an incredible community of recurring supporters. But, retention is the cornerstone of a sustainable monthly giving program. All of the growth ideas are meaningless if they don't stay with you.

That's why it's important to focus on making your supporters feel like they are part of the family.

YES! Don't be afraid to communicate with regular donors—and often.

Creating a family atmosphere among your supporters can be transformative. Before I jump into some case studies, here's a few ideas on how to welcome supporters into your organization's journey as you would a close-knit family.

→ **Share your struggles and challenges**—When you're open about the obstacles your organization faces, it invites supporters to be part of the highs and the lows. They'll understand the importance of their contributions and feel a deeper connection to your mission. Note: donors aren't inspired by all doom and gloom details; make sure to balance with hope and a way forward together.

→ **Celebrate milestones together**—Whether you've reached a fundraising goal, completed a project, or made a significant impact, sharing these achievements with your supporters strengthens the bond. It shows them the tangible results of their support and makes them feel valued. When there's an ask, donors are usually shown the problem, but they want to see small steps towards progress.

➜ **Personalize your communications**—Addressing your supporters by name and tailoring your messages to their interests and contributions makes a world of difference. Personalized communication shows that you see them as individuals, not just numbers, and that you appreciate their unique role in your mission.

➜ **Offer behind-the-scenes insights**—Giving your donors a peek behind the curtain—sharing stories from the field, introducing your team, and showing day-to-day operations—helps them feel like insiders. This transparency reinforces their importance to your work and deepens their engagement.

➜ **Engage in two-way communication**—Encouraging feedback and listening to your supporters' ideas and concerns creates meaningful dialogue. When donors feel heard and involved, it leads to stronger relationships and more dedicated support. This can be through email, social media, or a custom community channel if you've created one for your program.

➜ **Showcase their impact**—Regularly updating your donors on how their contributions are making a difference, using stories, photos, and videos, helps them see the direct results of their giving. This not only fulfills their sense of purpose but also reinforces their commitment to your cause.

- **Create a community**—Foster a sense of belonging among your supporters by organizing events, online forums, or social media groups where they can connect with each other and with your organization. When supporters feel like they're part of a larger movement, their commitment and loyalty grow.

By focusing on these elements, you can transform your supporters into a dedicated, loyal family, driving your mission forward and leading to higher retention rates.

If you're at the beginning stages of reworking your retention plan, **scan the QR code to get access to my 12-Month Plan for Joy & Gratitude** that shares some ideas and provides space to add in your own!

Now let's hear about a couple of programs that have activated very thoughtful joy and gratitude retention strategies!

RETENTION CASE STUDIES

Brown Bagging for Calgary's Kids (BB4CK): Hunger Heroes

500+ Monthly Donors | 90.7% Retention Rate

Mission: Ensure that no child in Calgary goes hungry.

There's no better place to start than with Lyndsey Enyimu, the Individual and Monthly Giving Coordinator at BB4CK. They've created an amazing twelve-month retention plan for their monthly program, Hunger Heroes.

BB4CK's mission is beautifully simple yet profoundly impactful: to ensure that no child in Calgary goes hungry. The organization is dedicated to providing healthy lunches to children who might otherwise go without. Every day, BB4CK prepares and delivers thousands of nutritious meals to schools and community partners, ensuring that kids have the food they need to learn, grow, and thrive.

Lyndsey explained, "We believe that every child deserves to have their basic needs met, and food is such a fundamental part of that. Hunger can affect a child's ability to concentrate, to learn, and to play. By providing these lunches, we're not just feeding kids; we're giving them the opportunity to succeed."

BB4CK's Hunger Heroes program was created in 2017 as a strategic initiative to ensure sustainable funding for its mission of providing nutritious lunches. Lyndsey and her team realized that one-time donations, while incredibly valuable, didn't provide the financial predictability needed for long-term planning.

From the start, BB4CK used compelling storytelling to connect potential donors to the impact of their contributions. They shared real stories of children who benefited from the lunch programs, emphasizing the difference a steady meal made in their academic performance and overall well-being. This narrative approach helped donors see the tangible outcomes of their monthly gifts, making them feel like active participants in the mission.

The Hunger Heroes program didn't just grow overnight. BB4CK consistently evaluated and adapted their approach based on donor feedback and engagement metrics. They invested in digital marketing and leveraged social media to reach a broader audience. By creating engaging online content and campaigns, they attracted new donors and retained existing ones, growing steadily to over 500 monthly donors with an average gift of $56.

Lyndsey said, "We wanted to make sure our donors feel as special as they truly are. They're not just contributors; they're heroes to these kids, and we need them to feel that every single month."

And let me tell you, they've crafted a plan that's all about spreading joy and gratitude!

Here's how it works:

1. **Monthly Storytelling and Updates:**

Every month, BB4CK sends out a beautifully crafted email that tells the story of one of the kids or families impacted by the donations. It's not just a generic thank you; it's a detailed narrative that brings the donors right into the heart of their mission.

Lyndsey mentioned, "We want our donors to see the faces and hear the stories of the children they're helping. It makes their contribution feel real and impactful."

Here's a sample of what their Sign-Up Automation Email Sequence looks like:

- Email 1: Welcome & Thank You—Executive Director says thank you for signing up to be a Hunger Hero and why sustainable giving is important.
- Email 2: Information about BB4CK—Stats about BB4CK and food insecurity with a graph. They also use this email to talk about the greater mission and vision.
- Email 3: Connection—Share a story.
- Email 4: Thank You & What's Next—Saying thank you again and for following along + what to expect next.

2. **Surprise and Delight Moments:**
Throughout the year, they surprise their donors with small tokens of appreciation. For instance, they send a little card

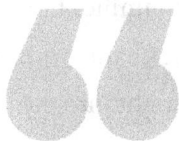

They're not just contributors; **they're heroes to these kids, and we need them to feel that every single month.**

Lyndsey Enyimu
Individual and Monthly Giving Coordinator
Brown Bagging for Calgary's Kids

with the number of lunches they provide each month, a handwritten thank-you card, and a colored brown bag.

3. **Special Recognition and Milestones:**
    BB4CK celebrates donor anniversaries and milestones in a big way. When someone hits their one-year mark as a Hunger Hero, they receive a personalized thank-you video from the team and a special magnet.

    "We're building a community," Lyndsey explained. "Acknowledging these milestones helps reinforce that they're a crucial part of our mission."

4. Engaging Events:

They also invite donors to exclusive events where they can see their impact firsthand. These might include virtual tours of the kitchen, meet-and-greets with the team, or even opportunities to help pack lunches.

5. Regular Impact Reports:

Twice a year, BB4CK sends out a detailed impact report. It's filled with statistics, success stories, and future plans, all designed to show donors exactly where their money is going and the difference it's making.

"Transparency is key," Lyndsey emphasized. "Our donors need to see the tangible results of their generosity."

It's clear that BB4CK's approach is all about creating a continuous loop of joy and gratitude. They've turned their monthly giving program into more than just a transaction;

it's a deeply personal and rewarding experience for everyone involved.

Lyndsey wrapped our conversation by saying, "Our goal is to make our donors feel like heroes every single month. We're so grateful for their support, and we want to make sure they know it, not just in words, but in heart-felt actions."

I love how thoughtful and personal their approach is!

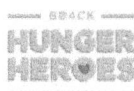

BB4CK

HUNGER
HEROES

NAME
ADDRESS
Calgary, AB
T2K 1P7

Happy Donorversary!

For the past year, you have been making a difference in the lives of the over 7,000 kids we feed every school day. Thank you!

You have officially been donating monthly for a year, which is truly amazing! You are part of a movement of over 500 Hunger Heroes, ensuring that kids in their communities are fed. The impact that our monthly donors have is immense.

Here is a quote from Deborah, one of the fantastic teachers who helps run the school's BB4CK lunch program in a school in the NE. She explained to me the impact our program has on the 65 students who rely on our lunches each school day:

"Having a full tummy allows them to learn and concentrate. I have seen many of these children make a 360 in behaviour, trust, and communication, all because we have food for them. Many parents face food insecurity at home. They can send their children to school knowing they will be loved and well-fed means so much. Students are in a place to learn, families are less burdened, and staff are able to do their job".

Talk about impact! Your monthly gifts help feed these kids, along with kids in more than 270 other schools across Calgary, nutritious lunches.

Every day, thousands of kids in our city still walk through their school's front doors without lunch in their backpacks. Your continuous support helps ensure they are fed.

Thank you for being a superhero! Please enjoy this small gift as a token of your continued support!

Lyndsey Enyimu
Individual & Monthly Giving Coordinator
lyndsey.enyimu@bb4ck.org

If you have any questions, would like to know more, or want a tour of our downtown kitchen, I would love to hear from you!

Scan this with your phone to find out about volunteer opportunities if you wanted to get involved in another way!

www.bb4ck.org

BB4CK
HUNGER HEROES

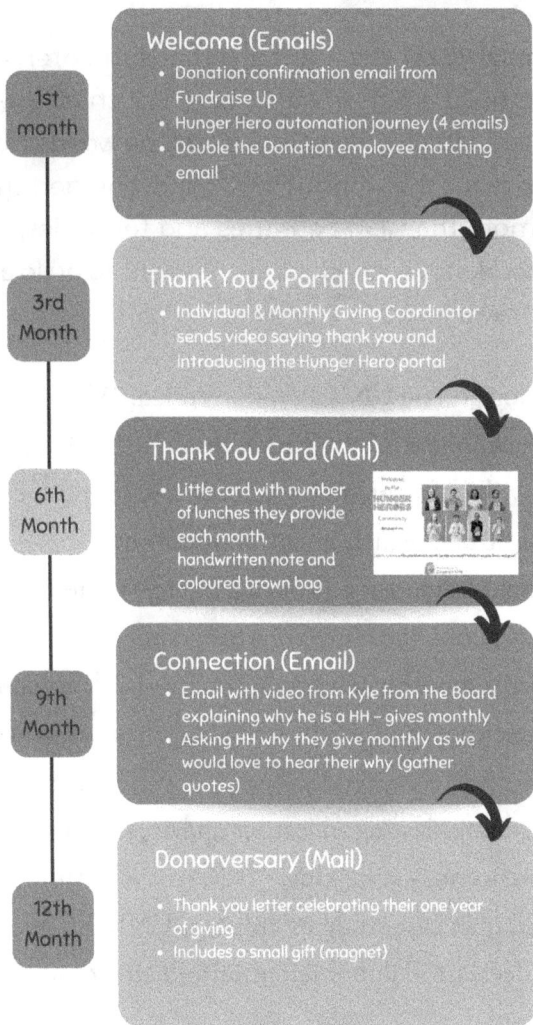

Welcome (Emails)

1st month

- Donation confirmation email from Fundraise Up
- Hunger Hero automation journey (4 emails)
- Double the Donation employee matching email

Thank You & Portal (Email)

3rd Month

- Individual & Monthly Giving Coordinator sends video saying thank you and introducing the Hunger Hero portal

Thank You Card (Mail)

6th Month

- Little card with number of lunches they provide each month, handwritten note and coloured brown bag

Connection (Email)

9th Month

- Email with video from Kyle from the Board explaining why he is a HH – gives monthly
- Asking HH why they give monthly as we would love to hear their why (gather quotes)

Donorversary (Mail)

12th Month

- Thank you letter celebrating their one year of giving
- Includes a small gift (magnet)

UNICEF

(Note: UNICEF wasn't an interview I conducted, so I don't have the exact statistics of their program, but I thought it was important to highlight how global organizations think through their recurring giving and personalization strategies.)

Mission: UNICEF, the United Nations Children's Fund, works to build a better world for every child, every day, everywhere. UNICEF works in some of the world's toughest places to reach the world's most disadvantaged children. Across more than 190 countries and territories, the UN agency works for every child, everywhere, to build a better world for everyone.

A 2020 blog post on UNICEF's site is titled: "Monthly Donors are the Backbone to UNICEF's Work." No doubt as an organization with global brand recognition and support, they have amassed a strong regular giving community.

It might seem even more of a challenge to create personalized touch points the more your program grows.

When a monthly gift hits someone's bank account, how can you recreate the initial feeling they had when they first clicked to give?

By communicating an impact update, sharing how much of a difference they're making.

Based on a case study by Infobip, UNICEF was experiencing a decrease in donor retention and an increase in churn with donors.

They had challenges on multiple fronts:

→ **Partial information:** They relied on various platforms for SMS, email, telemarketing, and WhatsApp to engage with donors. However, each channel operated independently, which created inconsistencies in the donor experience.

→ **Lack of communications data:** This fragmented approach hindered UNICEF's ability to effectively measure the performance of each channel. The lack of integrated performance metrics made it difficult to determine which communication methods were most effective in engaging donors.

→ **No email validation:** Although they achieved high delivery rates, the absence of proper email validation meant that many donors did not receive important retention content, ultimately affecting donor engagement and satisfaction.

To streamline donor communications and improve engagement, UNICEF embraced innovative tech and started to understand how their donors preferred to communicate. They worked with Infobip to create a digital-first omnichannel approach to build seamless and responsive communication with supporters.

In the blog post, UNICEF highlighted how this transformation allowed them to engage donors with personalized content and provide real-time updates on their projects. The case study mentioned the integration enabled UNICEF to send tailored messages at the right time, ensuring donors feel valued and informed. This personalized approach made donors feel more connected to the cause, leading to higher satisfaction and loyalty.

It also talked about how the platform's analytics and event-triggered messaging helped optimize their donor journeys. For instance, they could send welcome messages, thank-you notes, and updates based on specific donor actions. This kind of targeted communication was a big step up from their previous methods.

Overall, the switch to Infobip's platform helped UNICEF reduce donor churn by 33%, achieve a 7.8% increase in donor retention, and a 4% conversion rate on cart abandonment flow. It's a great example of how using the right technology can transform donor communication and retention efforts.

BB4CK and UNICEF are two examples of nonprofits making a conscious effort to make their supporters feel seen.

In Step 2: Make It Easy, we talked a lot about the tools and platforms on the front end to make the giving process seamless. It's also important to review the tech stack you need to scale, automate—*and personalize*—the continuous thank yous and updates.

Up next, we'll dive into a few common yet underutilized communication channels to take your joy and gratitude to the next level. There are many more, but here's a few that I'd consider applying to your strategy.

RETENTION TOOLS:

SMS aka Text Messaging

SMS is an extremely untapped and powerful tool in our sector as a retention strategy due to its high open rates, immediate delivery, and widespread reach. Look at your own communication on any given day. Are you mostly texting or calling people?

Almost every day, I typically receive at least one to three text messages from brands with a promotion. The only time I may receive texts from a nonprofit is usually on #GivingTuesday with an ask to donate and then poof! It's like the SMS strategy is gone.

Struggling with email open rates?

One of the most compelling reasons for nonprofits to use SMS is its exceptional open rate. Studies have shown that SMS messages have an open rate of 98%, with 90% of messages being read within three minutes of receipt! We're always on our phones.

Utilizing text messaging to send impact updates vs. fundraising asks is such a special touch that adds a very personal layer to your communication strategy.

I was recently at the Classy Collaborative in Chicago speaking with an old client of mine, the Gary Sinise Foundation.

The Gary Sinise Foundation's mission is all about giving back to America's heroes—our military members, veterans, first responders, and their families. They do a ton of great work, from building custom smart homes for wounded veterans to organizing fun and relaxing events for families and providing emergency financial help when it's needed. They're dedicated to making life a bit easier and brighter for those who've sacrificed so much for us.

We were chatting about their monthly donor program, and when the topic of retention efforts came up I threw out an idea that immediately created excitement around the table. What if your recurring supporters received a short audio text message directly from Gary Sinise every month with an update on the progress of different programs?

(If you're not familiar with Gary Sinise, he's a well-known American actor, director, and musician. You might recognize him from his iconic role as Lieutenant Dan Taylor in *Forrest Gump* or as astronaut Ken Mattingly in *Apollo 13*)

This is why an audio message would be so profound. Supporters are superfans of Gary!

I don't know about you, but if one of the organizations I support decided to send me an audio message through SMS or social media one day, that would not only MAKE my day, but I would feel so seen!

You might be thinking, but my donor base is older—will texting resonate?

Text messaging crosses all generations, and it's only increased in usage since COVID-19.

Vince PeGan, VP of Sales at Attentive, a personalized mobile messaging platform, noted that according to data from a major cellular carrier, there was a 26% rise in text messaging since the pandemic began. Additionally, consumer sign-ups for receiving text messages increased by 53%, reflecting a greater reliance on mobile communication.

A 2019 Pew Research Center survey of U.S. adults shows that over nine in ten Millennials (93%, ages 23 to 38), 90% of Gen Xers (ages 39 to 54), 68% of Baby Boomers (ages 55 to 73), and 40% of the Silent Generation (ages 74 to 91) own smartphones.

A huge chunk of them are avid texters. Even among those seventy and older, 94% are sending texts weekly.

My 71-year-old mom (hey mom!) texts me all the time. Gotta love the ones that end with "Love, Mom."

My recommendation? Test it!

Why does this matter for your nonprofit?

Simple: SMS is a cross-generational tool. Texting is quick, convenient, and perfect for reaching out to potential donors. So, don't overlook this powerful tool—Boomers are ready to text back and become a part of your mission!

There are many SMS platforms that allow for sophisticated data-driven personalization. You can segment your donor base and send tailored messages that resonate more deeply with individual supporters. This personalized approach can lead to higher engagement rates and more successful fundraising campaigns. According to Salesforce, personalized SMS messages can increase engagement rates by up to 50%.

Here's how I would think about using SMS messages in practice:

Let's pretend I have a monthly giving program called The Giggles (I have a fifteen-month-old, roll with me here) and the organization provides resources for new moms in underserved communities.

I would send:

- → Regular Updates
- → Personalized Messages
- → Engagement Opportunities
- → Milestone Celebrations

Regular Updates: Keep donors informed about how their contributions are being used—this can be by providing status updates on ongoing projects or in real time.

- → **Project Progress:** Short messages about the progress of ongoing projects.

  ### Example Project Progress Messages:

  "Hey [Donor Name]! Thanks to your support, we've provided 1,000 babies with formula this month. You're making a huge difference! :)"

  "Hey [Donor Name]! The new community center is halfway built! Thanks to your help, soon more moms will have a safe space to gather and learn."

  "Hi [Donor Name]! We've distributed 500 more baby care packages this week. Your support is bringing smiles to so many faces!"

➜ **Emergency Alerts:** Real-time alerts during emergencies, explaining how donor funds are being mobilized to provide immediate support.

Example Emergency Alerts:

"Urgent! Due to the recent storm, we're providing emergency supplies to affected families. Your donations are crucial right now. Thank you!"

"Alert! A sudden formula shortage is impacting our community. We're mobilizing quickly to help, thanks to your continuous support."

Personalized Messages: Make each donor feel recognized and valued. This personalization includes using the donor's name and referencing specific donation milestones.

Example Messages:

"Hi [Donor Name], your monthly support is transforming lives! Here's a story of how you've helped Sarah with her recent delivery of sweet Maggie."

"Hi [Donor Name], your monthly gift just helped Maria through a tough time with her newborn twins, Alex and Ana. Thank you for being there!"

"Hey [Donor Name], because of you, we've been able to support Jessica and baby Leo with essential resources. Your impact is incredible!"

Engagement Opportunities: Offer donors unique opportunities to engage more deeply with the organization's work. This includes invitations to virtual events, links to exclusive content, and prompts for further action.

Example Message:

"Join us for a live webinar to meet our latest moms! Click here to register: [link]"

"Exciting news, [Donor Name]! Join our virtual baby shower event next week. Meet the new moms and celebrate their journeys! [link]"

"Hi [Donor Name], we're hosting an exclusive Q&A with our founder this Friday. Come hear inspiring stories and ask your questions! [link]"

Milestone Celebrations: Recognize donor milestones to make them feel appreciated.

Example Messages:

"OMG happy 1-year anniversary! Thanks for giggling with us all year long! Did you know you're part of a community that's 3,017 strong? Together, you've collectively provided 25,000 babies with the essential items they need to grow healthy and strong."

"Wow, [Donor Name]! You've been with The Giggles for 6 months! Your support has changed countless lives. Here's to many more giggles together!"

"Hi [Donor Name], happy 2-year anniversary with The Giggles! You've helped us reach so many milestones. We're so grateful for your commitment!"

Now of course these would be sent with your brand voice, but it's important to humanize them. Think about how you text and what would feel like a natural fit to receive.

Feeling inspired to send some texts?

You've GOT MAIL

Emails are a foundation of any nonprofit's communication, offering a direct line to donors. Most donation tools send out an immediate email receipt—and shockingly that's often the only email that goes out after this transformational gift takes place.

It's really important to check the open rate and any click-through rates of the retention emails you send. Are people opening them? If not, it might not be the best channel to communicate with supporters, and you want to make sure they're hearing from you.

Your email best practices will differ based on numerous factors. It's not a one-size-fits-all solution; however, I've outlined two different strategies for small and larger organizations to test.

Email Marketing Plan for a Small Nonprofit

1. **Monthly Impact Newsletter**
   - Frequency: Monthly
   - Content: Updates on recent projects, success stories, upcoming events, and a call-to-action for donations.

       □ Example: A newsletter highlighting a recent project completion with before-and-after photos and a donor spotlight.

2. **Automated Welcome Series Post-Gift**
   - □ Frequency: Trigger-based (immediately after sign-up, followed by emails at day three, seven, fourteen, and thirty for a happy one-month anniversary email)
   - □ Content: Welcome message, mission overview, success stories, and how to get more involved.
   - □ Example: The initial email thanks the donor for joining, the second shares a story of impact, and subsequent emails provide ways to engage further.

3. **Quarterly Impact Report**
   - □ Frequency: Quarterly
   - □ Content: Detailed report on the nonprofit's achievements, financial transparency, and future goals.
   - □ Example: A report with infographics showing funds raised and how they were used. This can also be a video from your Executive Director or key stakeholder.

Email Marketing Strategy for a Larger Nonprofit (Team with Detailed Segmentation Capabilities)

1. **Weekly Updates**
   - Frequency: Weekly
   - Content: News updates, event reminders, volunteer opportunities, and donor highlights.
   - Segmentation: Tailor content based on donor interests and past engagement.
   - Example: Weekly impact stories and upcoming events tailored to different donor segments.

2. **Segmented Campaigns**
   - Frequency: Biweekly or as needed
   - Content: Customized messages for different regular donor segments (e.g., new, 1-2+ years, 5+ years, lapsed donors).
   - Example: Personalized emails that address specific donor journeys with exclusive updates or reengaging lapsed donors with a special campaign.

3. **Automated Donor Journeys**
   - Frequency: Trigger-based (varies by donor action)
   - Content: Within your emails, creating tags based on links people click on, creating different donor journeys to provide them with content they're interested in. (Not all email tools have this functionality, so it's a good question to ask if you're in the market of finding a new tool.)

◻   Example: You share your weekly update talking about three different projects your team is working on. I click on the school project, leading me to that blog. Now, you can tag me as interested in school projects and continue to send me updates just on that.

How can your email campaigns stand out?

When I signed up for Babylist to create my baby registry, I was asked to input my due date. Little did I know, this one piece of information would shape my entire experience with the platform.

As the weeks went by, I received personalized emails from Babylist, tailored to my baby's growth and development. They not only provided valuable information about my baby's progress but also suggested products that would be useful for certain phases. Even after Kennedy was born, the emails kept coming, guiding me through each growth leap and recommending products that would make the journey easier.

All of this was possible because of that one key data point I had provided from the beginning. Just imagine: a single detail can make such a significant difference. What if you could create a custom experience for your supporters based on one special data point? The possibilities are endless.

What's your special data point? The one that can help you create a personalized experience for your supporters. Don't underestimate the power of a single detail. It could be the key to providing an unforgettable, impactful experience.

EMAIL FREQUENCY

If you've ever been afraid of sending TOO many emails, let Daily Giving help prove otherwise.

Every day their supporters receive an email that expresses where funds are going.

Every. Single. Day.

And as a refresher, they have 15,000+ monthly donors.

Their next retention initiative is for all supporters to receive a phone call between three and six weeks after their gift from another daily giver, thanking them for getting involved. So cool, right?

Instead of strictly following recommendations from Google, MailChimp, or Constant Contact, focus on what feels right and natural for your program's structure and purpose. Tailor your communication strategy to fit your unique goals and audience, ensuring it aligns with the core values and objectives of your monthly giving initiative.

There's been weeks where I don't send a single email and weeks where I send four or multiple in one day. Think through the strategy and what cadence makes sense based on what you're trying to accomplish.

One Black Friday weekend (no longer just a day of promotions), I received 12+ emails from Nespresso. Yes, I love coffee. I didn't open many of them, but because of the multitude of emails they remained top of mind and once I had the time in my day, I opened one and made a purchase.

Even sending an email and having your name in someone's inbox, whether it's opened or not, generates brand awareness. Many nonprofits tend to err on sending less emails rather than more in fear of unsubscribes.

You know what, welcome those who unsubscribe because they weren't in it for the long haul anyway. Buh-bye!

The next strategy to share joy and gratitude isn't a direct communication channel, but one that when created makes a supporter's experience as a regular donor with you stand out.

SURPRISE & DELIGHT MOMENTS

One of my favorite personal surprise and delight moments came in 2023 from being a member of Dressember's Collective.

I received an email on February 23, 2023, with the subject line: *These exclusive perks could be yours.*

Naturally, I'm inclined to see what's inside. They were running a campaign to incentivize new people to join the Collective.

Inside it read:

Join Our Community of Year-Round World Changers

Looking for a way to fight trafficking year-round? The Dressember Collective is a community of committed monthly supporters who ensure we have the resources to protect vulnerable populations at risk of trafficking, provide a pathway out for victims, and empower survivors year-round. Monthly giving is a simple, consistent way that you can use your resources to end human trafficking around the world.

Our appreciation for the Dressember Collective is too great for words: we're gifting all members a hip pack from MADE FREE° as a token of our gratitude. All Collective members—old and new!—are eligible to claim this gift in March. Each MADE FREE° hip pack[4] helps people obtain self-sustaining jobs and gives hope and opportunity for a life to be made free from human trafficking and poverty.

Then another email was sent out to only Collective members asking us to fill out a Google Form with our address and to select the color of the hip pack.

Now, there was no need to do this. Most people aren't giving because they get a gift in return.

However, what's brilliant about this is it's a values-aligned partnership with MADE FREE, and it's a bag I now wear pretty much every time I exit the house and go on trips. Whenever I'm stopped and asked about it, I can share the story of Dressember and that I'm part of The Collective.

Is there an anniversary, a special day of the year, a donor's birthday, or a random Tuesday where you can

---

4   A hip pack is a crossbody bag or fanny pack for us '80s babies.

create a surprise and delight moment? It doesn't have to be a tangible item.

Here are a few other ideas that can add a special touch:

1. **Personalized Thank-You Videos:** Nonprofits like charity: water send personalized thank-you videos from the field, showing donors the direct impact of their contributions. Seeing the beneficiaries and hearing their stories can be incredibly moving and personal.

2. **Exclusive Access:** Some organizations offer exclusive access to virtual events, behind-the-scenes tours, or webinars with key staff members or special guests, providing donors with an insider's view of the nonprofit's work.

3. **Custom Artwork or Gifts:** Nonprofits may send small tokens of appreciation, such as custom artwork created by the beneficiaries or unique gifts related to the nonprofit's mission. For example, an animal rescue might send a photo and paw print of a rescued animal, or a conservation nonprofit may send a postcard with a beautiful image of a protected area.

4. **Surprise Donations:** Occasionally matching the monthly donations of their supporters for a month or providing an additional donation to a related cause on behalf of the donors, showing that their support is even more impactful.

5. **Donor Recognition:** Featuring donor names on the nonprofit's website, annual report, or donor wall, recognizing

their ongoing support and contributions to the organization's success.

Monthly Giving mastermind Alumni Liza Nugent from Maloto sent me their recent annual report and not only did the brochure feature their monthly donor program, The Table, but they had a full page dedicated to all the recurring supporters and the impact that community has made together.

6. **Special Experiences:** Inviting monthly donors to special events, such as galas, project launches, or field visits where they can see the impact of their donations firsthand and meet the people their contributions are helping.

These surprise and delight moments help strengthen the relationship between nonprofits and their monthly donors, making them feel more connected and appreciated, ultimately leading to increased retention and support.

Are your wheels spinning about new retention methods to constantly share joy and gratitude? Yay! These are all ideas for you to devise what will work best for you and your team, whether you're just starting out or looking for something more robust.

Try something out, give it time to perform, check the data, and revise.

Join me in the last chapter where we'll discuss the future and hear advice from organizations doing the work right now.

AHA Moments!

1. **Focus on Appreciation Over Acquisition:** In our quest for growth, we often prioritize acquiring new supporters. However, shifting our focus to retaining and nurturing existing supporters can be far more impactful. It's the loyal supporters who consistently contribute and believe in your cause, making a sustained difference. By emphasizing "thank yous" instead of "will yous," you can build deeper, more meaningful connections with your current supporters.

2. **Personalize the Supporter Experience:** Retention is the cornerstone of a sustainable monthly giving program. To achieve higher retention rates, make your supporters feel like part of the family. Share your organization's struggles and successes with them. Provide regular updates on how their contributions are making a difference in the way they'd prefer. Email, SMS, phone call? As you scale, an omni-channel approach will be important, leading to higher satisfaction and loyalty among your supporters.

3. **Celebrate Milestones and Show Gratitude:** Recognize and celebrate your supporters' anniversaries and milestones. This could be through personalized thank-you videos, special recognition items, or exclusive events. For instance, Brown Bagging for Calgary's Kids (BB4CK) sends personalized thank-you videos and special magnets to donors who reach

their one-year mark. Such gestures reinforce the importance of each supporter and make them feel valued and appreciated.

4. **Use Consistent and Transparent Communication:** Keep your supporters engaged with regular, transparent communication. No ghosting! This includes sending monthly storytelling updates, surprise and delight moments, and detailed impact reports. This level of transparency helps supporters see the tangible results of their generosity, strengthening their connection to your cause.

5. **Check Your Churn Rate:** Take a look at your current churn numbers. Do you notice any trends? Remember when I referenced Recurly earlier and how in 2023 alone, they helped clients recover over $1.2 billion in revenue that could have been lost due to payment issues! If you're experiencing churn due to credit cards expiring and not having the proper tech stack to follow up, start making notes to talk to your technology partner about what's possible.

NEXT STEPS:

_____

_____

_____

_____

_____

_____

_____

_____

CHAPTER 11
The Future

SO, WHERE DO you go from here?

You just read incredible case studies from organizations of all sizes outlining how the 5-Step Framework works in practice. Emphasis on "in practice." Yes, I hope this book inspires you but also creates action.

I'd recommend starting with a Monthly Giving Audit.

Review each of the steps below, and this will help you identify areas that need improvement or make necessary changes. Look at the data, identify any patterns or gaps, and determine areas that need to be updated. This will give you a clear understanding of where to focus your efforts.

Once you have identified areas for improvement, it might feel overwhelming to tackle everything at once. By taking it slow and steady, you will see the positive impact of the 5-Step Framework on your organization's giving program. This will ensure that each change is implemented effectively and allows you to track the impact of each change.

Change can be daunting, but it's necessary for growth. As you implement the framework, be open to new ideas and willing to take risks. Innovation often comes from stepping outside of your comfort zone and trying something new.

Take it one step at a time.

One change at a time.

One improvement at a time.

If you're curious which platforms and tools will help YOU start or scale at this current moment, I've put together a list of "Recommended Monthly Giving Platforms & Tools" at positiveequation.com/book. Scan the code here to access!

I hope this serves as a blueprint for the incredible product you're about to build.

Your believers are waiting to be invited in. :)

THE MONTHLY GIVING AUDIT

Create The Product

➔ What's your leadership and organization's stance on recurring giving?

➔ What's the reason behind it?

➔ Does the existing structure make sense?

➔ Do you view it and treat it as a product?

➔ Do you have a name?

Take it one step at a time.

One change at a time.

One improvement at a time.

Notes

Make It Easy

→ Is your donation process seamless?

→ Do you have a well-designed, accessible website specifically for the program?

→ Do you have the proper tech stack to ensure flexibility for supporters to manage their regular gifts?

Notes

Call in the Believers

➜ How are you calling in your existing community and finding new superfans?

➜ Are your leadership and staff leveraging personal stories?

➜ Do you provide some creative freedom on how supporters can share your message?

➜ Is the copy clear and inclusive on all marketing fronts?

➜ Who are your corporate partners that can amplify the program?

Notes

_____

_____

_____

_____

_____

_____

_____

Make the Ask

➜ Where does monthly giving live on your priority of asks?

➜ What stories are you sharing, how are you sharing them, and who is telling them?

➜ Do you have a strategic plan throughout the year when you're making asks?

➜ Have you created upsell opportunities for existing supporters?

Notes

_____

_____

_____

_____

_____

_____

_____

Constant Joy & Gratitude

→ What's your current retention plan to say thank you often?

→ How can you make someone feel seen?

→ Are you using channels where your donors communicate? (SMS, social)

Notes

_____

_____

_____

_____

_____

_____

_____

_____

By focusing on these elements, you can enhance your organization's ability to attract and retain monthly donors, ensuring a steady stream of support and a sustainable impact on your mission. Now, take these insights, apply them to your strategy, and watch your monthly giving program flourish!

As a mastermind, we're here to help each other through this together. Not just with the tactics and ideas but with motivation and encouragement as well.

A question I asked everyone I interviewed was, "**What's your advice for organizations looking to grow their monthly giving efforts?**"

Here's what they had to say.

CLARITY AND IMPACT

Gloria Umanah, The Hope Booth:

"Get as clear about the ask and impact ratio as possible. It's helpful to show that this dollar amount means this impact. Go hard at it. Phone calls worked for us, so we went hard with phone calls to lock in support."

LEVERAGING PERSONAL CONNECTIONS

Cubby Graham, charity: water:

"You need to reach new people, and often ads can help. But referrals are powerful. Each member of The Spring has a unique referral page. People who hear about us from friends or family are more likely to join because they trust the source."

SETTING GOALS AND CAPACITY

Marissa Marx, Dressember (now IJM):

"Set clear goals and ensure your team has the capacity to manage the program. It involves ops, comms, and development working together to run it smoothly."

TRYING NEW APPROACHES

Hannah Braly, Because International:

"Don't be afraid to try new things. Even if a campaign isn't initially successful, you can learn and adapt. Transparency and honesty about where the money goes are crucial."

QUANTIFYING SUCCESS

Brittany Friedner, Feeding Westchester:

"Track the performance of campaigns. For example, a $10,000 investment in telemarketing for monthly giving brought in over $60,000. Demonstrating lifetime value is essential to gaining trust and securing future investments."

EMBRACING IMPERFECTION

Cyndi Otteson, Miry's List:

"Just mess around and find out. Nothing is going to be perfect from the start. Start with what you have and iterate."

STEWARDSHIP AND RELATIONSHIP BUILDING

Lyndsey Enyimu, BB4CK:

"Research is crucial. Connect with other nonprofits to learn best practices. Stewardship is key—get to know your donors and keep communication consistent."

PSYCHOLOGICAL EASE

Arieh Friedner, Daily Giving:

"People are willing to give more over time in smaller intervals because it's psychologically easier. Creating a culture of giving and consistency is vital."

BUILDING AUDIENCE AND OPPORTUNITY

Kyle Roosen, Tim Tebow Foundation:

"It doesn't matter how great your monthly giving program is if you don't have anyone to talk to. Build your audience consistently and offer compelling opportunities for them to join."

FOCUSING ON RELATIONSHIPS

Kebo Drew, QWOCMAP:

"Fundraising is a group activity. Engaging board members and motivating donors to share their experiences strengthens your program."

STARTING EARLY

Jessica Campbell, Chamber of Mothers:

"The best time to start a monthly giving program was 10 years ago. It takes time to build, so start now to see long-term benefits."

HOLISTIC APPROACH

Meghan Walsh, Roots Ethiopia:

"Bringing together all the elements of a monthly giving program—video, platform, clear messaging—into a cohesive strategy is crucial for success."

As we look ahead, it's clear that the evolution of the subscription economy will shape the future of recurring giving in exciting and transformative ways.

I also asked the organizations, **"How do you see monthly giving evolving within consumer giving?"** Here are some key insights and quotes from your peers, recapped to highlight emerging trends and future directions.

BEYOND FINANCIAL CONTRIBUTIONS

Gloria Umanah from the Hope Booth emphasized the growing desire for deeper involvement. She sees monthly giving evolving beyond financial donations to include time, resources, and personal connections. "People want to do more than just give; they want to be a part of the work. Creating opportunities for them to engage beyond dollars is crucial," she noted. Gloria imagines a future where donors might even offer their homes for team retreats, illustrating the limitless possibilities of donor engagement.

CONTENT IS KING

Cubby Graham from charity: water highlighted the importance of content. "People subscribe to Spotify for music and Netflix for content. For our monthly giving program, it's the stories and exclusive content that keep people engaged." He believes the future lies in providing compelling content that inspires and connects donors to the cause on a deeper level. "We're doubling down on producing more content for our community," Cubby shared.

THE SHIFT TOWARDS CORE FOCUS

Becky Straw from The Adventure Project pointed out that monthly giving is becoming a central focus for many nonprofits. "It's just the way that people prefer to give. It's easier to scale and forecast." She also mentioned the need for better data management tools, reflecting on the limitations she's encountered with current CRM systems. "We need more sophisticated data to track and optimize monthly giving," she explained.

CONVENIENCE AND ACCESSIBILITY

Lyndsey Enyimu from BB4CK emphasized the convenience and accessibility of monthly giving. "People like the ease of giving monthly. With the digital payment options available today, it's become simpler to contribute regularly." She noted that younger donors, in particular, appreciate payment methods like Apple Pay and Google Pay, which facilitate hassle-free giving.

PERSONAL ATTRIBUTION

Arieh Friedner from Daily Giving discussed the personal attribution of monthly donations. "We're seeing a shift towards a mindset where giving is part of their identity." He highlighted how this approach helps in building a culture of consistent and committed giving.

ENHANCING THE DONOR EXPERIENCE

Kyle Roosen from Tim Tebow Foundation (TTF) believes that nonprofits need to create joyful giving experiences. "We can learn a lot from e-commerce about creating positive online experiences. It's about making donors feel the impact of their contributions and connecting them to the mission." He emphasized using digital tools to enhance transparency and build a sense of community among donors. "It should be the best experience and most fun thing that we do online is that we get to choose what we have impact with. How do we really help supporters feel the return on your investment, the return on impact?"

COMPETITIVE DIFFERENTIATION

Dean Gillespie from IJM UK talked about the need for nonprofits to differentiate themselves in a crowded market. "It's not enough to just be a nice charity. We need to add tangible value to the donor experience." Personalized engagement and leveraging artificial intelligence are essential to optimize fundraising efforts. "AI can help us better understand donor behaviors and tailor our approaches accordingly," Dean explained.

I don't have a crystal ball; however, in all of my discussions and research, here's where I'd place my bet:

1. **More Personalization with AI**—Imagine a world where everything you subscribe to feels tailor-made just for you. More advanced than quizzes where you enter your information to get a result. I believe we're heading there, thanks to AI. These smart systems will analyze your preferences and behaviors to offer experiences that fit you perfectly. More than just personalized donation amounts, nonprofit technology will use AI to send you personalized updates and engagement opportunities that make you feel truly connected to the cause.

2. **Easier Payments, More Data & Reporting Options**—Most donation tools are getting better and better at this. In the next few years, standard payment options, including stock donor-advised fund (DAF), etc., will make it simpler to support your favorite causes. CRM platforms will get smarter and provide more reporting specifically around recurring. I envision CRMs will have strategic recurring KPIs (key performing indictors) built into the reporting like donor churn rate, cost per acquisition, etc. Some of this already exists with more robust platforms like Virtuous.

3. **Subscription Bundles**—We're all familiar with subscrip-
    tion bundles in entertainment—like getting Disney+,
    Hulu, and ESPN+ together. This idea will expand to other
    sectors, including nonprofits. Imagine donating monthly to
    one organization and it unlocks this multipartnership with
    other brands to receive exclusive content, event invites,
    and more, all in one package. This approach adds value
    and keeps you engaged longer. (Hint: great conversation
    to have with corporate partners!)

4. **Experiential Opportunities to Meet Your Commu-
    nity**—Subscriptions will go beyond products and services,
    focusing on real-life and virtual experiences. Nonprofits
    might offer virtual or in-person events, volunteer oppor-
    tunities, and meet and greets with staff as part of their
    subscription models. This creates a deeper emotional bond
    and makes you feel like part of a community.

5. **Integration with Smart Devices**—The Internet of Things
    (IoT) will play a big role in future subscriptions. Think of
    smart home devices automatically reordering products or
    managing subscriptions based on your usage. Nonprofits
    can use IoT to send real-time updates and engagement
    opportunities, making your experience even more interac-
    tive and timely.

The next five to ten years will see the subscription economy
becoming more personalized, flexible, and community-focused.
Nonprofits can harness these trends to create more engaging

and impactful experiences for their supporters, making it easier and more rewarding.

This book might be ending, but your journey is just beginning.

Building a robust monthly giving program takes time, effort, and a willingness to adapt. Use the 5-Step Framework as your guide, but remember that every organization is unique. Tailor your approach to fit your mission, your needs, and your supporters.

YOUR FINAL NEXT STEPS

1. **Audit Your Program:** Evaluate where you are now and identify areas for improvement.
2. **Take Action:** Implement changes one step at a time, track your progress, and don't forget to celebrate your successes!
3. **Join the Community:** Get an automatic group of accountability partners and continue learning and growing together in The Sustainers Slack channel.

The mastermind has just begun…

Welcome to your #MonthyGivingEra.

Let's make a difference together, one month at a time.

FEATURED MONTHLY GIVING PROGRAMS

SO GRATEFUL FOR the organizations that said "Yes!" to sharing their personal journeys and taking us behind-the-scenes of their monthly giving programs.

Each organization is linked at positiveequation.com/book to visit their websites, learn more about each mission, and connect with their teams.

1. charity: water—The Spring
2. Dressember—The Collective
3. Because International—The Sole
4. Feeding Westchester—Nourishing Neighbors
5. Miry's List—Welcomer's Circle
6. The Adventure Project—The Collective
7. Brown Bagging for Calgary's Kids—Hunger Heroes
8. The Water Project—The Water Promise Circle
9. Daily Giving
10. Tim Tebow Foundation—The Movement and The Defenders

11. IJM UK—Freedom Partners
12. Queer Women of Color Media Arts Project
13. The Hope Booth—The Movement
14. Chamber of Mothers—The Matriarchy
15. Roots Ethiopia—The Roots

BIBLIOGRAPHY

INTRO

1. National Council of Nonprofits. (n.d.). *Economic Impact of Nonprofits*. Retrieved from https://www.councilofnonprofits.org/about-americas-nonprofits/economic-impact-nonprofits

2. BWF. (2024). *Giving USA 2024 Report Insights*. Retrieved from https://www.bwf.com/giving-usa-2024-report-insights/

CHAPTER 1: SETTING THE STAGE

1. Fundraising Effectiveness Project. (2019). "2019 Annual Survey Report." Association of Fundraising Professionals. Available at: https://afpglobal.org/sites/default/files/attachments/generic/FEP2019AnnualSurveyReport.pdf

2. CauseVox. "Top 4 Donor Retention Strategies To Keep Donors For Life." Available at: https://www.causevox.com/blog/top-donor-retention-strategies

3. Classy. (n.d.). Storytelling Tips to Boost Recurring Donations. Retrieved from https://www.classy.org/blog/storytelling-tips-boost-recurring-donations

CHAPTER 3: SUBSCRIPTIONS FOR GOOD

1.   Wikipedia contributors. (2024, June 19). *Book of the Month*. In Wikipedia, The Free Encyclopedia. Retrieved from https://en.wikipedia.org/wiki/Book_of_the_Month

2.   Encyclopedia.com. (n.d.). *Book-of-the-Month Club*. Retrieved from https://www.encyclopedia.com/media/encyclopedias-almanacs-transcripts-and-maps/book-month-club

3.   Ries, S. (2020, June 30). A History of Book of the Month Club. *Book Riot*. Retrieved from https://bookriot.com/history-of-book-of-the-month-club/

4.   "National Society for the Prevention of Cruelty to Children," *The Oxford Companion to British History*. Encyclopedia.com, May 15, 2024. Retrieved from Encyclopedia.com.

5.   Muslic, H. (2017, October 27). *A Brief History of Nonprofit Organizations*. Nonprofit Hub. Retrieved from https://nonprofithub.org/a-brief-history-of-nonprofit-organizations/

6.   GivingTuesday Data Commons. (n.d.). *Fundraising Effectiveness Project Report*. Retrieved from https://data.givingtuesday.org/fep-report/

7.   Neon One. (n.d.). *Recurring Giving Report*. Retrieved from https://neonone.com/resources/recurring-giving-report/

8.   Tzuo, T. (2016). *The Subscription Economy and the Future of Business*. Zuora. Retrieved from https://www.zuora.com/wp-content/uploads/2016/09/ceo_mag2_9_02_16_tzuo.pdf

9.   Tzuo, T., & Weisert, G. (2018). *Subscribed: Why the Subscription Model Will Be Your Company's Future—and What to Do About It*. Portfolio.

10.   Who Gives A Crap. (n.d.). *Who Gives A Crap*. Retrieved from https://us.whogivesacrap.org/

11. Imperfect Foods. (n.d.). *Imperfect Foods*. Retrieved from https://www.imperfectfoods.com/

12. Netflix. (n.d.). *About Netflix*. Retrieved from https://about.netflix.com/en

13. Robinson, C. (2024, March 9). *Subscription Service Model: How To Build A Profitable Business*. Forbes. Retrieved from https://www.forbes.com/sites/cherylrobinson/2024/03/09/subscription-service-model-how-to-build-a-profitable-business/

14. Chargebee. (2024). *2024 State of Subscriptions: Revenue Growth Insights*. Retrieved from https://www.chargebee.com/blog/2024-state-subscriptions-revenue-growth-insights/#:~:text=2024%20and%20beyond.-,Subscription%20revenue%20projected%20to%20increase,confidence%20in%20the%20subscription%20economy.

15. Gneezy, U., Imas, A., Brown, A., Nelson, L. D., & Norton, M. I. (2012). *Altruism and the Self*. Journal of Economic Perspectives, 26(1), 133-144.

16. Dunn, E. W., Aknin, L. B., & Norton, M. I. (2008). *The Psychology of Giving*. Science, 319(5870), 1687-1688.

17. Moll, J., Krueger, F., Zahn, R., Pardini, M., de Oliveira-Souza, R., & Grafman, J. (2006). *The Neural Basis of Human Altruism*. Annals of the New York Academy of Sciences, 1119(1), 36-57.

18. UpScribe. (n.d.). *From SaaS to Stitch Fix: A Look Back at the History of the Subscription Model*. Retrieved from https://www.upscribe.io/blog/from-saas-to-stitchfix-a-look-back-at-the-history-of-the-subscription-model/#:~:text=One%20of%20the%20earliest%20documented,publications%20on%20a%20regular%20basis.

19. Recurly. (2024, January 16). *Recurly Recovers $1.2 Billion in Subscription Revenue for Its Customers in 2023*.

Retrieved from https://recurly.com/press/
recurly-recovers-one-point-two-billion-dollars-in-
subscription-revenue-for-its-customers-in-2023/
#:~:text=SAN%20FRANCISCO%20%E2%80%93%20
January%2016%2C%202024,its%20customers%20around%20
the%20globe.

CHAPTER 4: GROWTH MINDSET

1.   Wondery. (n.d.). *Netflix vs. Blockbuster: Sudden Death*.
      Business Wars. Retrieved from https://wondery.com/shows/
      business-wars/episode/5296-netflix-vs-blockbuster-sudden-death/

2.   Worthy, C. (2021). *Change Enthusiasm: How to
      Harness the Power of Emotion for Leadership and
      Success*(p.189). Hay House.

3.   BetterWorks. (n.d.). *Cassandra Worthy: Major Changes Serve
      Your Evolution*. Retrieved from https://www.betterworks.com/
      magazine/cassandra-worthy-major-changes-serve-your-evolution/

CHAPTER 5: THE 5-STEP FRAMEWORK TO BUILD, GROW, & SUSTAIN SUBSCRIPTIONS FOR GOOD

1.   PhotoSecrets. (n.d.). *The Rise and Fall of Kodak*. Retrieved
      from https://www.photosecrets.com/the-rise-and-fall-of-kodak

2.   KPBS. (2014, May 19). *San Diego Opera Will Not Close,
      Announces 2015 Season*. Retrieved from https://www.kpbs.
      org/news/arts-culture/2014/05/19/san-diego-opera-will-not-clos
      e-announces-2015-seas

3.   Schoenberg, N. (2012, January 23). *Chicago's Hull House Closes
      Its Doors: Time to Revive the Settlement Model?*. The Nation.
      Retrieved from https://www.thenation.com/article/archive/
      chicagos-hull-house-closes-its-doors-time-revive-settlement-model/

4.   Dressember. (n.d.). *Our Story*. Retrieved from https://www.
      dressember.org/story

CHAPTER 6: CREATE THE PRODUCT

1.   Kelly Jeep Chrysler. (2024, April 12). *The Story Behind Those
      Jeep Ducks*. Retrieved from https://www.kellyjeepchrys-
      ler.net/blog/2024/april/12/story-behind-those-jeep-ducks.
      htm#:~:text=A%20woman%20named%20Allision%20
      Parliament,all%20needed%20during%20the%20pandemic.

2.   Reader's Digest Editors. (2023, June 20). *The Heartwarm-
      ing Story Behind Jeep Ducks*. Reader's Digest. Retrieved from
      https://www.rd.com/article/jeep-ducks/

3.   MotorTrend Editors. (2023, July 28). *Duck, Duck, Jeep: The
      Viral Trend That's Bringing Joy to Jeep Owners Everywhere*.
      MotorTrend. Retrieved from https://www.motortrend.com/
      features/duck-duck-jeep/

CHAPTER 7: MAKE IT EASY

1.   Donorbox. (n.d.). *Nonprofit Statistics You Must Know*.
      Retrieved from https://donorbox.org/nonprofit-blog/
      nonprofit-statistics

2.   Cherry, K. (2023, May 11). *How Herd Mentality Explains Our
      Behavior*. Verywell Mind. Retrieved from https://www.verywell-
      mind.com/how-herd-mentality-explains-our-behavior-7487018

3.   Shopify. (2024, June 7). *16 Strong Abandoned Cart Email
      Examples*. Retrieved from https://www.shopify.com/blog/
      abandoned-cart-emails

4.   Klaviyo. (n.d.). *Abandoned Cart Emails: Best Practices and
      Examples to Boost Your Revenue*. Retrieved from https://www.
      klaviyo.com/blog/abandoned-cart-email

5.   Klaviyo. (n.d.). *Abandoned Cart Benchmarks: What Good
      Performance Looks Like in 2024*. Retrieved from https://www.
      klaviyo.com/blog/abandoned-cart-benchmarks

CHAPTER 8: CALL IN THE BELIEVERS

1.   Evans, B. (2023, June 14). *SEC, Big Ten each collect
      more than $2 billion in athletics revenue, dwarfing rest
      of Power Five*. USA Today. Retrieved from https://
      www.usatoday.com/story/sports/college/2023/06/14/
      sec-big-ten-2-billion-athletics-revenue-power-five/70313053007/

2.   Davis, S. (2023, June 15). *Ohio State Athletics Made $252M in
      2022 Revenue; Texas, Alabama Among Top Schools*. Bleacher
      Report. Retrieved from https://bleacherreport.com/articles/100
      79336-ohio-state-athletics-made-252m-in-2022-revenue-texas-a
      labama-among-top-schools

3.   Business of Story. (n.d.). *The 10 Brand Story Elements
      of REI's Disruptive #OptOutside Black Friday
      Campaign*. Retrieved from https://businessofstory.com/
      the-10-brand-story-elements-of-reis-disruptive-optoutside-bl
      ack-friday-campaign/

4.   Movember. (n.d.). *Team* 2420649. Retrieved from https://
      us.movember.com/team/2420649

5.   Movember. (n.d.). *Team* 11815989. Retrieved from https://
      us.movember.com/mospace/11815989

6.   Movember. (n.d.). *Team* 14762724. Retrieved from https://
      uk.movember.com/mospace/14762724

7.   Creativeo. (2023, February 21). *StoryBrand One-Liner
      Examples*. Retrieved from https://www.creativeo.co/post/
      storybrand-one-liner-examples

8.   World Wide Web Consortium (W3C). (2018). Web Content
      Accessibility Guidelines (WCAG) 2.1. Retrieved from https://
      www.w3.org/TR/WCAG21/

9.   IKEA Foundation. (2015, March 24). *Better Shelter: IKEA Foundation and UNHCR Ready to Improve Life for Thousands of Refugee Families*. Retrieved from https://ikeafoundation.org/press/better-shelter-ikea-foundation-and-unhcr-ready-to-improve-life-for-thousands-of-refugee-families/

10.   Seva Foundation. (n.d.). *TOMS: Partnering for Sight*. Retrieved from https://www.seva.org/site/SPageNavigator/programs/toms

11.   Taco Bell. (n.d.). *Taco Bell Foundation for Teens Partners with Boys and Girls Clubs of America*. Retrieved from https://www.tacobell.com/news/taco-bell-foundation-for-teens-boys-and-girls-clubs-of-america

CHAPTER 9: MAKE THE ASK

1.   Alexander, J. (2019, September 19). *MoviePass is shutting down: a timeline of the company's rise and fall*. The Verge. Retrieved from https://www.theverge.com/2019/9/19/20872984/moviepass-shutdown-subscription-movies-helios-matheson-ted-farnsworth-explainer

2.   Soho House. (n.d.). *About Us*. Retrieved from https://www.sohohouse.com/en-us/about

3.   DonorPerfect. (n.d.). *Five Reasons Why a Monthly Giving Program Will Benefit Your Organization*. The Chronicle of Philanthropy. Retrieved from https://www.philanthropy.com/paid-content/donorperfect/five-reasons-why-a-monthly-giving-program-will-benefit-your-organization

CHAPTER 10: SHARE CONSTANT JOY & GRATITUDE

1.   Infobip. (n.d.). *UNICEF: Creating a Better Future for Children with Advanced Messaging Solutions*. Retrieved from https://www.infobip.com/customer/unicef

2.   Pew Research Center. (2019, September 9). *U.S. Gen-erations and Technology Use.* Retrieved from https://www.pewresearch.org/short-reads/2019/09/09/us-generations-technology-use/#:~:text=More%20than%20nine%2Din%2Dten,Center%20survey%20of%20U.S.%20adults

3.   Attentive. (2023, June 7). *How to Master Multigen-erational Marketing Using Personalized Text Messag-ing.* Retrieved from https://www.attentive.com/blog/how-to-master-multigenerational-marketing-using-personalized-text-messaging

4.   Statista. (n.d.). *Forecast of Mobile Phone Users Worldwide*. Retrieved from https://www.statista.com/statistics/274774/forecast-of-mobile-phone-users-worldwide/

5.   Mosio. (n.d.). *Text Messaging, Older Demographics and Clinical Research*. Retrieved May 28, 2024, from Mosio website.

ABOUT THE AUTHOR

Dana Snyder is the founder of Positive Equation, a sought-after keynote speaker and workshop facilitator, author, host of the acclaimed global podcast "Missions to Movements", and creator of the Monthly Giving Mastermind. Her mission is to empower nonprofits to attract supporters through innovative digital marketing and to create sustainable giving models by establishing recurring giving programs, making philanthropy accessible to all. Dana was recently named one of the Top 100 Nonprofit Influencers shaping change in the sector. Based in Atlanta, she enjoys spending her time traveling and exploring with her husband, daughter, and labradoodle.